Church Club of New York

The Church in the British Isles

Sketches of its Continuous History from the Earliest Times to the Restoration

Church Club of New York

The Church in the British Isles
Sketches of its Continuous History from the Earliest Times to the Restoration

ISBN/EAN: 9783337412715

Printed in Europe, USA, Canada, Australia, Japan

Cover: Foto ©Lupo / pixelio.de

More available books at **www.hansebooks.com**

THE CHURCH

IN

THE BRITISH ISLES

Sketches

OF ITS CONTINUOUS HISTORY

FROM

THE EARLIEST TIMES TO THE RESTORATION

LECTURES DELIVERED IN 1889 UNDER THE AUSPICES OF THE
CHURCH CLUB OF NEW YORK

THIRD EDITION

NEW YORK
E. & J. B. YOUNG & CO.
COOPER UNION, FOURTH AVENUE
1893

CONTENTS.

PAGE

LECTURE I.

THE CELTIC CHURCH.. 1
  The Right Rev. Wm. C. Doane, D.D., S.T.D., LL.D.,
  Bishop of Albany.

LECTURE II.

THE ANGLO-SAXON CHURCH...................................... 61
  The Rev. Samuel Hart, D.D., Professor of Latin
  at Trinity College, Hartford.

LECTURE III.

THE NORMAN PERIOD.. 97
  The Rev. Alex. V. G. Allen, D.D., Professor of Ecclesiastical
  History at the Theological School, Cambridge.

LECTURE IV.

THE REFORMATION PERIOD....................................... 157
  The Right Rev. H. T Kingdon, D.D., Bishop Coadjutor
  of Fredericton, New Brunswick.

LECTURE V.

THE PURITAN REACTION.. 201
  The Rev. Thomas F. Gailor, S.T.B., Professor of Ecclesias-
  tical History at the University of the South.

PREFACE.

Those who in theory or in practice deny that corporate union of Christians is desirable, undervalue one of the main functions of the Church, albeit one which has for some centuries been but imperfectly fulfilled; that is, its witness, as a continuous institution, to the verity of the facts of Christianity. An unorganized number of believers, of different confessions, without external or visible association, are witnesses each to his own experience or belief; and the force of their testimony lies in the concurrence of so many persons.

The Church's existence as an institution is evidence of a different kind. This indicates both the experience or the belief of the individuals who now constitute the organization and the prevalence of that belief when the organization was founded.

It carries back the testimony to contemporaneous witnesses who saw the facts that they declared, and it has perpetuated their testimony, making it speak afresh to each successive generation of men. No other institution has exerted so profound an influence upon human society, and none has shown so wonderful adaptability to the vicissitudes of human experience both social and individual, and no other has maintained its essential character and its vital principles without change or diminution, as this has; and to-day it is witness to the same facts that it testified to eighteen centuries and a half ago.

The corporate organization of the Church has alone made this testimony possible. It has both preserved the formal statement of the Christian faith, and checked individual and sectary deviations from it. Whilst most of the important evangelical bodies of Christians have held to the same facts in general, and even to the form in which the Church declares them, however far they may have departed from the Church's unity and order, and from her ministry and sacraments, yet who shall say that the Catholic Church's standard has not been their guide? that she has not really marked the channel of the truth, however they may have seemed to be steering their own way? Suppose that at and after the time of the Reformation all Christians had deserted the Church, as so many did in Northern Europe and Great Britain, and had established all over Christendom little or large sects, or independent congregations, each with its own confession, its self-constituted ministry, and its own pride of opinion: would they not have lost themselves and been swallowed up, like the Rhine, in the sands and swamps of philosophical and theological uncertainties, of political and social transformations?

As in all human affairs the most cogent evidence of past transactions is found in their monuments, whether in the chipped flints of cave-dwellers, the pyramids of Egyptian kings, or the jurisprudence of Justinian, so we, confronted by the monuments of Christianity—the Church, with her sacraments and holy rites, the Lord's Day, and others, and by the effects of Christianity upon mankind,—we believe that Jesus Christ lived, and died, and rose again, and was what He declared Himself to be, the Eternal Son of God.

An invisible Church has no such evidential value. It has neither form nor organization, no connection with the past; it is not a monument nor an institution; it is, in short, not a thing at all: it is but an idea, a philosophical conception, a name. It is not a house built of hewn stones: it is a heap of pebbles.

As time separates the generations of men farther and farther from the events of our Lord's life on earth, the importance of maintaining this monument in all its strength increases; and Churchmen deplore the weakening of this evidence of Christianity by Christians, whose chief interest has too often seemed to be its disparagement. Impressed with this need the Bishops of the whole Anglican Communion have invited all Christians to return to the unity of the Catholic Church, and have named the four well-known propositions on the basis of which this result may be achieved, namely the Scriptures, the Creeds, the Sacraments, the Historic Episcopate.

Organized soon after the General Convention of 1886, in which these overtures were promulgated by the House of Bishops, the Church Club set on foot a course of lectures with a view to elucidate in some measure the significance of the last of these points, the Historic Episcopate, not so much in the form of a critical study as in the form of a popular exposition of the teaching and practice of the Church on this subject during the period that intervened between the Ascension of our Lord and the first General Council of Nicæa, in A.D. 325, when the form of the Creed was substantially settled; a period during which the teaching and practice of the Church is in theory, if not actually, appealed to with confidence by nearly all Christians as the true standard of uncorrupt Christian faith and theology, and by which most of the educated reformers and founders of sects professed to be guided. In those lectures, delivered by the Bishops of Western New York and Springfield, and by Professors Richey, Garrison and Egar, the remarkable consensus of the great fathers and teachers of the Church, and of the Church's practice everywhere was very strikingly portrayed; and incidentally they forcibly illustrated the possibility of theologians and communities of widely differing habits of thought and life, dwelling in far-distant lands, or near together, placing special stress on different points of the Christian faith, and contending as the special champions of one or another phase of the truth, without setting up a new sect, or cutting loose from the Catholic Church, in order to give emphasis to their particular topics: an example which, if the piety of Protestants had followed it, would have gone far to preserve the unity of the Church to our own days.

That course of lectures has been followed by another, of which the present volume contains the first series, designed to exhibit the continuous corporate life in the British Isles, of the Church whose teaching and practice were thus described, not by a discussion of the evidence of continuous succession of the Episcopate, but by describing in brief sketches how the British and English Church, the stock and parent of the Church in the United States, appeared and acted in the great periods and larger divisions of her history, in relation to the State, the individual, and the Church in other lands, and how she fulfilled, at different times, her divine mission to the people who dwelt in those islands; and so sketching our biography back to the Apostolic ages. The second series of this course, continuing the history to the present day, will soon be published.

The thanks of the Church Club and of Churchmen are due to the lecturers, Bishops Doane and Kingdon and Professors Allen, Hart and Gailor, whose learned and careful coöperation has enabled the Club to carry out the scheme of these lectures.

Ascension Day, 1890.

The Celtic Church.

LECTURE I.

THE RT. REV. W. CROSWELL DOANE, S.T.D., LL.D.,
Bishop of Albany.

THE CELTIC CHURCH.

I THINK I may be justified in assuming that I am here to speak not *to*, but in *the name* of the Church Club: that I am not expected to say much that is new to the instructed intelligence of thoughtful Churchmen; but rather to help them in setting before those who have not been called upon to look into the story—at any rate, from our standpoint,—the grounds of our conclusion about the cradle of Christianity in which our ecclesiastical babyhood was really rocked, and about those who rocked that cradle when the Church and the religion of Jesus Christ were in their infancy in Britain.

And having said this, I think it right to say one more thing: that I am sure it is important, even at the risk of some tedious repetition of well-known facts, to avoid what is said (I think with justice) to be a clerical error—namely, the taking for granted that the people whom we are teaching know as much about the subjects as the teachers themselves.

One must frankly say, in reference to the story of the first missionaries to that which was the original of England, that it is enveloped in the impenetrable mystery of myths; and the mystery of myths, like the mists that veil the inaccessible mountains, and muster their shadow-fleet upon the marge and rim of the mighty sea, are of double birth—earthy and heavenly; springing from beneath, but drawn up on high. Whatever may be the human admixture in the ten separate legends as to the first evangelization of Britain, there is at least the heavenly element in them of high motive and holy zeal. And myths mean always distance and expanse. So that even if St. Clement's description of St. Paul's journey, "to the boundary of the setting sun," shall only mean Spain and the Gauls; if the story of the consecration, by St. Paul, of Aristobulus means merely what the name means, that the *best counsel* and judgment were used and set apart for this great work; if the holy thorn of Glastonbury, instead of being an Aaron's rod, fades into a dry stick without either leaf or bloom; if we must give up the story in the Welch Triads of the father of Caractacus, coming back, like Onesimus, from his exile as a hostage to be a preacher of the faith;

if we must forego Bede's story of the mission of Lucius to Eleutherus, the Bishop of Rome (till it means only that Rome was *free* to act for the conversion of these heathen); even if we relegate all these to the shadowy land of legends, at least there is evidence in their very shadowiness of the very early introduction of Christianity into Britain, before history becomes legible, or chronology troubles itself with dates.

Loveliest and most unlikely of the fabulous foundings of Christianity in Britain is the story of Glastonbury. One almost hates to say that no evidence of it existed earlier than the eleventh century. It has so tinged the romantic history of the period, and is so closely connected with the favorite hero of knighthood and chivalry, King Arthur; and it has been recited in so many stories of wandering minstrels, and sung itself in such sweet idylls in Tennyson and Lowell, that, false and foolish as the story is, it seems to have had in it a power of purity and a motive of high purpose, in a very peculiar period of English history. When Sir Galahad, the just and faithful knight of God, whose "strength was as the strength of ten, because his heart was pure," rides "unarmed whate'er betide until he finds the Holy Grail," we must remember that it was the story of the introduction of Christianity into England by Joseph of Arimathea, through which the element of religious chivalry entered into the court and times of Arthur, whose knightly vow was "to break the heathen and uphold the Christ." St. Joseph was reported to have brought with him the San Greal or Sang Real, the sacred chalice of the first Eucharist, or the cup in which the Angels collected the drops of blood during the crucifixion; and the story of this vision, granted to the maiden knight, rings in our ears and lingers in our hearts with at least this holy teaching: that the vision of God is to the pure in heart; that only high and holy consecration can preserve manhood or womanhood against the temptations of the flesh; and that they only and they always, to their souls' good, find in the chalice of every Eucharist the true Blood of Christ, who come to the holy Altar with pure and clean hearts.

It is a curious phase of this legend that at the councils of Pisa and Constance and Basle, the question of precedence between English and French ambassadors came constantly up, and finally was decided in favor of the English ambassador, on the ground that the English traced their Christianity to Joseph of Arimathea, who came earlier to Britain than Dionysius the Areopagite came to France.

To be told that the source of a great river is inaccessible, because the way to it lies through the tangle of primeval forests, because its crystal cup is concealed by the accumulation of the dry leaves of countless Novembers, is at least to know that the stream takes its rise in a region of primitive purity, and is incorrupt and uncontaminated at the fountain head.

There must be in any investigation like this a certain agreement about the meaning of unusual words; a certain recognition of facts of profane history and legend; and a certain amount of knowledge of the connection among the nations, at the true beginning of European history, or we cannot intelligently enter upon the fascinating subject of this lecture.

To begin with, let us understand that by the term Celtic Church, we mean the Church which existed in Great Britain and Ireland five centuries before, and as many centuries after, the mission of St. Augustine. In central England, before Augustine landed, the Church had become extinct, partly by the extermination of its members, and partly by the removal of the rest to a safe distance from the heathen invaders. In North Wales, Scotland and Ireland the Britons remained, differing from the usages and independent of the rule of the Anglo-Saxon Church, until the close of the eighth century, and in Cornwall until the close of the tenth. So that we *must* (rather we *may*) include in this survey the story, in a portion at least of Great Britain, of at least eight centuries of Christian life and work. Equally important it is to recognize certain facts of profane history, about the people whom we call the Celts, and about their relation to the inhabitants of other countries. Celts, Galatians, Gauls: these are the same words really, in their root; and the relation among these people, in their different dwelling places, was close, and is important to be studied. The oldest form of the name undoubtedly is Celt, which we find in Dionysius and Strabo, in Hecataeus and Herodotus It was the name by which the Gauls in the neighborhood of Marseilles designated themselves. Later on they were called by the Greeks Galatians; and the Roman name for the same people was the Gauls.

Originating in Central Asia, one of the three great divisions of men (Celts, Teutons and Slavs), they were a restless, turbulent, nomad people, retaining their characteristics in spite of admixtures, whether with the Phrygians and Greeks in Asia, with Romans and Jews in Gaul, or in England, with Saxons, Normans and Danes.

Lightfoot in his wonderful introduction to the Epistle of the Galatians describes them as " quick of apprehension, prompt in action, very impressible, and with a great craving after knowledge," and on the other hand, as " constantly quarrelsome and treacherous in their dealings, incapable of sustained effort, and very easily disheartened by failure." " The language in which Roman writers speak of the martial courage of the Gauls [he quotes Livy], impetuous at the first onset, but rapidly melting in the heat of the fray, well describes the short-lived prowess of these converts in the warfare of the Christian Church," and while Cæsar speaks of them as " very much given to religion," Motley says, in his " Dutch Republic," that "the Celtic element from the earliest ages had always been keenly alive to the more sensuous and splendid manifestations of the devotional principle."

Giving over the vain attempt to disentangle fact from fable, in the earlier accounts of the emigration of these people from Asia into Britain, it is at least certain that in the century before the Christian era a portion of the Celtic group had settled in Britain; and when Julius Cæsar landed (fifty-four years before Christ) Wales and Cornwall and the South of England were peopled by them.

There are historians, and especially in our own day, who have attempted to find in the religious rites and philosophy of the Druids, who were the priests of heathen Britain, certain lines of providential preparation for the introduction of Christianity. And though Lightfoot does not hesitate to say that "the nobler aspect of the Druidical system has been exaggerated," there certainly were some points of teaching, eminently their doctrine of the immortality of the soul, which left the people who held it upon a higher plane than was attained by even such philosophers as Marcus Aurelius, or by the religions of the Roman world.

So much for the character of the people. If we are puzzled about the date and circumstances of the first population of Britain by the Celts, we shall find ourselves even more at sea in attempting to fix the precise time or manner of the introduction of the faith of Christ among them. I suppose it may be taken as a recognized fact to-day that the earliest *unquestionable* statement of the existence of Christianity in Britain is in " Tertullian Against the Jews," about A.D. 207. " The different nations of the Gauls and the portions of Britain inaccessible to the Romans, have been truly conquered for Christ." An argument of certainly ingenious plausibility, I think one may almost say of possibility, carries us back thirty years further. The Asiatic mission of Pothinus and Irenaeus to the Church in Gaul would naturally have found vent in the direction of Britain. This would be about the year 176, and although in Irenaeus' enumeration of the countries in which the one true faith was professed (in his book " Against the Heresies ") no specific mention is made of Britain, it is not impossible that he included the Britons among the Celts in Gaul; more possible because in the list of the Bishops present at the Council of Arles (A.D. 314) the three British Bishops who were there are catalogued among the Bishops of Gaul. There is still another possibility, which has in it the ring and character of Apostolic times, when the persecution that arose about Stephen scattered the disciples to become σπερμολογὸι, "sowers of the word," in the various countries to which they fled for shelter. It is not impossible that the terrific persecution, under the Emperor Marcus Aurelius in A.D. 177, drove Christians from southern Gaul to Britain, who carried with them the message of the Master, to which they became witnesses in life, as their brethren at Vienne and Lyons had been witnesses for it unto death; and so the blood of Gallican martyrs became the seed of the British Church. What Mr. Pryce calls "the surprising ductility with which Christianity crept through the various pores of the world" may perhaps after all be the true account of the introduction of the religion of Christ into Britain. Put two things together. Remember the statement which Tertullian made of his own time (which was true long before his time) that "Christians filled every place, cities, fortresses and towns, and even the camps." And remember that in A.D. 61, twenty years after London was founded, it was a flourishing town, with a commerce that connected the Thames with the Mediterranean; and it is quite possible that, as in southern Gaul so in Britain, the truth was brought early, and found lodgment and growth before the first century was over.

"Thus," Bishop Lightfoot says, "in the age when St. Paul preached, a native of Galatia spoke a language essentially the same with that which was current in the southern part of Britain. And if (to indulge a passing fancy) we picture to ourselves one of his Asiatic converts visiting the far West to barter the hair-cloths of his native country for the useful metal which was the special product of this island, we can imagine that, finding a medium of communication in a common language, he may have sown the first seeds of the Gospel, and laid the foundations of the earliest Church in Britain."

It is impossible to pass in silence over the well authenticated facts of the story of the Church's early life and work in Gaul. There is not wanting authority for the opinion that when St. Paul wrote to Timothy that "Crescens had gone to Galatia" it was the European and not the Asiatic country to which he went. At any rate the Churches at Vienne claim him as their founder. This of course would place the date of the first planting of Christianity in Gaul not long after the middle of the first century. And it is true that Pothinus, a friend of Polycarp, who was St. John's disciple, became Bishop of Lyons; and that Irenaeus became the great preacher to the native population of this city. Leaving to others the ministry of the wealthier and more cultivated Greek and Roman population, he set himself to the study of the Celtic language that they might hear " in their own tongue the wonderful works of God." And the pathetic story of the persecution which overwhelmed those converts in Lyons and Vienne, as they told it themselves in their letter to their brethren in Asia Minor, proves the reality of their conversion and the constancy of their faith.

We do not forget either the Provincial Synod at Lyons, with twelve Bishops present, in the middle of the second century; nor the fact that it was on his march through Gaul that Constantine embraced Christianity. The same century produced the great Bishop of Tours, St. Martin, " the Apostle of Gaul," whose fame and influence are commemorated alike by St. Ninian's " Candida Casa," or Whitehouse, the stone church built at what is known as Whithern in Scotland; and by the oldest surviving church in England, St. Martin's in Canterbury, which still retains in its walls some of the old Roman bricks of the chapel in which Ethelbert's Queen Bertha worshipped; and where Ethelbert permitted Augustine and his monks to worship with her; and where, on Whitsunday in A.D. 597, he was himself baptized, the first of the Saxon kings to embrace the religion of Britain, which for nearly five centuries had existed in the kingdom.

I really think that this Galatian element is perhaps the most vital feature in the Celtic story. It is most important to recognize that so far as the grace of Orders is concerned, it matters not one whit whether they came through Rome or from the East. No error of doctrine, no viciousness of life affects in the faintest degree the validity of transmitted grace, any more than the moss that greens the outside, or the decay that softens the bark, of wooden troughs vitiates the clearness of the water, or destroys the purity of the spring from which the water flows. But it is so striking as to seem at least providential that, as the first introduction of Christian belief and life leaked over from Gaul, according to the earliest genuine records; so the Saxon line, which twined its authority in with the old Apostolic network, came from the Bishop of Arles in France, whose descent is Ephesine and so Eastern; and Johannine and not *Roman at all.

We have noticed Tertullian's statement in the beginning of the third century, of the subjugation of the remote parts of this island to Christ. Origen, writing in A.D. 239, argues for the greatness of the Christian religion from its diffusion through the whole world, and specifies, in evidence, the

* I do not say *Petrine;* because even if it were Roman, it would have no special relation to St. Peter, who was never Bishop of Rome.

fact that it had reached the Moors and "the Britons who are divided from our world." And there is similar testimony from Eusebius and Hilary. Arthur Haddan, in his remarkable review called "The Churches of the British Confession," is inclined to consider that, "during all these early centuries and almost until the departure of the Romans, Christianity was confined to Roman settlements and Romanized natives, and limited to the Roman provinces of Britain with no national strength or character; only a feeble reflection of its Gallic sister across the channel, from whom almost certainly it was derived." But the difficulty of either accepting or rejecting this conclusion is found in the acknowledgment by Gildas, the first British historian, that "if there were any early records of his own country, they had been destroyed in the fires or had been conveyed by his exiled countrymen to foreign lands." He wrote in 576; and through and from his statement we are able to pass on sure and safe grounds. The Roman occupation of Britain lasted for about three hundred years. The Picts were never subdued by Roman arms. And when, in the opening of the fifth century, the Roman legions were withdrawn from Britain, the land was given over to three separate invaders, the Picts from the Highlands, the Scots, as they were called, from Ireland; and the Saxon pirates. Attacked on four sides, north, west, east and south, the problem remained unsolved for nearly a century, as to what race should finally dominate the island. The hiring of mercenaries, the pitting of barbarian against barbarian, the slow surrender, the bitter resistance, the hiding behind the fastnesses of mountains and the thicknesses of woods, all these are matters of well known history. And at last Saxons and Jutes having only partially conquered, the outcome was that the Engles became the final conquerors and Britain really became England. "The new England may well be called a heathen country." Green, in his "History of the English People," puts most strongly the relation of these events to the history of the Celtic Church.

"Before the landing of the English in Britain, the Christian Church stretched in an unbroken line across western Europe to the farthest coasts of Ireland. The conquest of Britain by the pagan English thrust a wedge of heathendom into the heart of this great communion, and broke it into two unequal parts. On the one side lay Italy, Spain and Gaul, whose Churches owed obedience to and remained in direct contact with the See of Rome. On the other side, practically cut off from the general body of Christendom, lay the Church of Ireland. While the vigor of Christianity in Italy and Gaul and Spain was exhausted in a bare struggle for life, Ireland which remained unscourged by invaders, drew from its conversion an energy such as it has never known since. For a time it seemed as if the course of the world's history was to be changed, as if the older Celtic race that the Roman and German had swept before them, had turned to the moral conquest of their conqueror; as if Celtic and not Latin Christianity was to mould the destinies of the Churches of the West." And Haddan says, " Church historians cannot be far wrong in saying that a mere turn of the scale, humanly speaking, prevented the establishment in the seventh century of an aggregate of Churches in north-western Europe, looking for their centre to the Irish and British Churches, and as entirely independent of the papacy as are the English-speaking Churches of the present day. The Celtic skull and the Celtic temperament, we are told by naturalistic ethnologists, are perforce Romanist. We commend the fact to notice, that the largest and most powerful company of European orthodox Churches, not paying obedience to the Roman See at any period anterior to the Reformation, consisted of the entire aggregate of the Celtic Churches existing at the time, with the addition of a body of Celtic missions among Teutonic tribes." That turn of the scale, it is plain to see, was due in the first place to the lack of any real unity among the inhabitants of the British islands, who were divided into separate and contending races and tribes; and to their entire severance from southern Christendom, which led them to look rather to Jerusalem and the Holy Land than to Rome. And while, as we shall see later on, great missionary enterprises were undertaken into the lands across the sea, the wave of Christianity was constantly passing to and fro, as Ireland gives St. Columba to Scotland, and Scotland gives St. Patrick to Ireland; and as the religion of the Master, beaten back from one point established itself among the inhabitants of some remoter portion of the land. It was as though a full spring disappeared from one locality to pour its waters in another place; as though the sunlight hidden by some overhanging cloud left the centre of a landscape in shade, to dispense its glory on some distant scene.

I hope I have at least guarded against three popular mistakes. One, that unless St. Paul went to Britain, there is no evidence whatever as to the source from which it derived its Christianity; one, that if there is no evidence of the source, then there is no proof that Christianity existed in Great Britain in the earlier days; and one, that the first planting of the religion of Christ dates from the landing at Canterbury of the Monk Augustine in A.D. 597.

While on the one hand we recognize that Celtic Christianity, overborne by the wave of English heathenism, was hardly to be found in southern

England; yet let us remember that the queen who welcomed Gregory's messenger with such cordial affection, and won him access to her husband, was a descendant herself from one of those Christian kings in the line of Clovis of France; so that even when the tide of Italian missions touched the English coast, it met the wave of Galatian Christianity; and the two mingling into one made the Christianity of Great Britain, like its civilization, composite, but with its dominant element still Galatian and Eastern. And I hope that I have not only cleared up the confusion in so many minds on this subject, but that I have impressed my hearers with the fact that from whatever source derived, and to whatever space extended, the Celts of the first century had heard of and trusted in Christ; that probably this was true not merely of Roman settlements and Romanized natives, but of the Celts themselves, speaking the common language, and learning in it the common faith of their brethren, first in Asiatic, and then in European Gaul; that while authenticated history hardly begins until the time of Gildas, indisputable evidence from the writings of the third century prove that Christianity was certainly in Britain a well known and established fact, in the century before; that the organization of the Church was Apostolic in its government by Bishops, if not in its founding by one of the

Apostles; that it was Catholic, in that it derived its orders from, and held communion with, the Church of Christ in Jerusalem and Italy and Spain and France; that its Bishops were recognized, as representing an organized and independent national Church, at Arles and Sardica, if not at Nicea; that it was so filled with the spirit of Christ and His Apostles, that it perpetually set itself to conquer for Christ its barbarous and heathen conquerors; that it was finally, and most strongly, established in Ireland, because Ireland was free from the scourge of perpetual invasions; and that we must recognize as thorough an independence in the Church of the Scots (as the Irish people were called then) and the Celts and the Britons, as exists to-day in the English Church, the successor of the Anglo-Saxon organization, which, in the eleventh century, absorbed into itself the national and ecclesiastical organizations of Scotland, Ireland, England and Wales.

May I say one more thing about the character of this old Mother Church of ours? Namely, that it vindicated alike its catholicity, its holiness, its unity, and its Apostolic origin by its orthodoxy. Here again two facts are constantly overstated and misunderstood. It is true that certain British Bishops, when nearly all Christendom was touched with the plague of Arianism, signed a semi-Arian creed at Ariminum in 359;

and it is true that Pelagius was a Briton and that his heresy spread for a while among his fellow-countrymen. But we have distinguished and venerable evidence, from St. Hilary, St. Athanasius, St. Chrysostom and St. Jerome, in the earlier centuries (I mean the fourth and fifth), that the British Church, in the language of St. Athanasius, " had signified their adhesion to the doctrine of the Nicene Creed." Montalembert allows, with regard to primitive Ireland, what is I think proven in regard to the whole Celtic Church, that " it was profoundly and unchangeably Catholic in doctrine, but separated from Rome in various points of discipline and liturgy."

It is one of the grave mistakes into which men have been drawn in the heat of controversy to call the Celtic Church *anti*-Roman. The very title is an anachronism. Founded and flourishing in the days when the Bishops of Rome claimed only local and suburbicarian jurisdiction, she was, like every ancient, independent Church, *un*-Roman. At the time of her founding, Rome itself was virtually a Greek Church. The fact of the existence, propagation, and extension of the Celtic Church, through centuries when communication with southern Europe was impossible; of her Bishops recognizing and recognized by, the Church in Rome as everywhere else; and of their stubborn refusal to submit to any intrusive jurisdiction, are simply illustrations of that traditional independence which for so many centuries was universal in the world. That the old See of central and civil prominence was held in honour, but *second* to Jerusalem; that Bishops, in many instances, got consecration and mission, but not jurisdiction from the Bishop of Rome, is undoubtedly true: but no one can read the story of the attitude of Columbanus toward Boniface IV., or of the British Bishops who held conferences with St. Augustine, and not realize the absolute autonomy of the Church, whose Bishops wrote such words and maintained such an attitude toward Rome.

Although their connection is more in subject than in time, let me put these two things together here. Columbanus, one of the Irish saints at the end of the sixth century (he was Bishop of Leinster), writes to Boniface IV. lamenting over " the infamy of the chair of St. Peter in consequence of disputes at Rome," urges him to " be more on the watch and to cleanse the See from all error"; says that " many persons entertained doubts about the purity of his faith"; allows " Rome to be the chief city of the world and of the Church, save the especial prerogative of Jerusalem"; and upbraids the Roman Church " for claiming a greater authority and power than was possessed by other Churches"; all in language which can, by no excess of ingenuity be reconciled with any claim of papal supremacy. And the attitude of the British Bishops toward Augustine at the two conferences, due in part to national antagonism and to an unwillingness to recognize a Pope at home in Canterbury, nevertheless proves that no such claim of authority, as Rome made in England in the later years and makes now over all the Churches in the world, was known or acknowledged in Britain. In the same way, I think, too much has been made as to the difference between Britain and the rest of the Western churches in regard to the keeping of Easter. About the time of the council of Nice the practice of the British Church harmonized with that of the entire Western Church; but after that time the Britons, probably as Bede says, "because the synodal decrees about the time of the observance of Easter did not reach them owing to their distant position," fell into the observance of a different day, by adhering to the old cycle known as that of Sulpicius Severus. It is a mistake to imagine that they adopted the quarto-deciman theory, or that their position grew out of their Eastern Galatian source and sympathies; but the mere fact that they went on for so many centuries independently of, and differing from, the Roman use, shows that no connection between England and Italy was needful to keep up the orthodoxy or the order of the Church. What Maclear says of the conquests of Cæsar is true in a deeper ecclesiastical sense. He is speaking of the fact that Ireland and Scotland were exempt from the invasion of the soldiers of Cæsar, and he says " Britain never became *quite* Roman as Gaul did ; and Ireland was never Roman at all." Would that the latter were true now; and thank God for the strong statement we can make to-day about England.

The other differences were as to the method of administering baptism, which may have been and probably was, that they baptized with the *single* immersion against the Apostolic canon; and the consecration of Bishops by a single Bishop.

Surely it cannot but be providential that in so many ways,—at the beginning, in times of national severance, in times of restoration,—the English Church, from British days to our own, has been independent of, even when in full communion with, the Roman See; in Galatian origin; in Gallican orders and liturgy; in the strong link twice fastened, through Lyons and Arles, with Ephesus and St. John, and in the striking facts that Ninian, her first great missionary, and Aidan, the restorer of St. Augustine's ruined work, and Germanus, the defender of the faith against Pelagius, all came, with no mission and no authority from Rome.

It happens not unfrequently that history is written best in the lives of the men who made it. Among the crowd and confusion of events as they melt into the indistinctness of distance, here and there stand out solitary and conspicuous figures, who were in part the incarnation of the spirit of the age, and in part the spirit that informed the age. I think one may really learn more, of some distinct and most characteristic periods of Celtic Church history, in the lives of St. Patrick and St. Columba, of St. Aidan and St. Margaret, both associated with Columba, than in almost any other way. Of course I am passing over many prominent and attractive names which loom out from the darkness of the pagan background, and the almost darker confusion of legend and romance; like St. Ninian, a British Christian, consecrated by St. Martin of Tours, who became the Apostle of the Southern Picts, and built the stone church at Galway, in the early part of the fifth century; St. Kentigern, who followed in Ninian's footsteps, and is known in Glasgow as St. Mungo, because of "the gentleness and sweetness" of his nature; of St. Aidan, who, Bishop Lightfoot says, was the true Apostle of England, because God gave to him the privilege of restoring what was left of "St. Augustine's Mission in England." Many others there are of whom one may say with St. Paul that "the time would fail him to tell." But the four names that I have mentioned have such clear personality, and cover such important periods of history that they may be well considered as representatives of their time.

The story of St. Patrick comes to us beset and surrounded with peculiar difficulties. Bede, who records the coming of Palladius, the first Bishop sent to "the Scots believing in Christ," is absolutely silent concerning St. Patrick. It is to be noted here first, that the Scots were the people of Ireland; and that the historian's statement that "they believed in Christ" recognizes the existence of Christianity there before he came. And it is further to be recognized that Patrick came apparently without any commission from the then Pope Celestine. Columbanus, the Bishop of Leinster (which St. Ninian founded) never alludes to him at all; and no single writer before the eighth century makes more than passing mention of him; and makes no reference whatever to the story of Marianus Scotus (who died in 1084) that "after preaching for sixty years, St. Patrick converted the whole island of Ireland to the faith." At the same time, St. Patrick's "Confession," as it is called, and his curious letter to Coroticus (both of which are counted genuine) give evidence of the fact and reality of his mission, and tell the leading particulars of his life.

He was born about 387, not only of Christian

parentage, but his father was a Deacon and his grandfather a Priest. He was twice taken captive by the pagans and carried to Ireland, where he lived in captivity and was employed in tending sheep. Earnest and enthusiastic in his nature, he dwelt much in his solitary life upon religious matters and especially upon what he calls " the disobedience of his fellow-countrymen to God, and to the Priests who admonished them for their salvation." And in this rapt condition of feeling he felt his vocation to the Ministry, coming to him in a vision and through a voice which he could not disobey. " In the dead of the night," he says, " I saw a man coming to me, bearing innumerable epistles, and he gave me one of them and I read the beginning of it which contained the words ' the voice of the Irish,' and I heard in my mind the voice of those who were near the wood Folocut which is near the Western Sea." " And again on another night, I know not, God knoweth, whether it was within me or near me, I heard distinctly words which I could not understand except that at the end of what was said there was uttered, ' He who gave His life for thee is He who speaketh with thee.' And so I awoke rejoicing." Against the entreaties of his relatives and friends he seems to have gone to the monastery of St. Martin at Tours, and studied under St. Germanus and afterward at Lerins, whose famous school is best known through its distinguished scholar Vincentius.

Although his consecration has been connected with the then Bishop of Rome, Celestine, there is no evidence for it, and the most natural supposition is that he was consecrated Bishop where he was ordained Priest, by the Bishops of Gaul.

The only name that he associates with his mission is that of Victor, the man who appeared to him in the vision, and his only statement of himself in his letter to Coroticus is " Patricius, a sinner and unlearned, but appointed a Bishop in Ireland." He probably landed in the north part of the County of Wicklow, and traversed the country, in his mission, over its whole extent.

Stripped of what Skene calls the *encrustations* of legendary matters, he seems to have ordained large numbers of clergy, of whom an unusual proportion were Bishops after the manner of that period. Angus the Culdee says that there were "three hundred and fifty Bishops and three hundred presbyters"; the Bishops many of them being of the nature of the Chorepiscopi. Mr. Skene describes it as "a congregational and tribal Episcopacy." And the fact that the chief king of Ireland remained a pagan during all of St. Patrick's mission, goes to show that at least there was never any national adoption of Christianity. He established a large number of monastic schools and devoted himself with great courage and labour, to breaking down alike the idolatrous paganism of the country, and the nature worship which to a large extent prevailed.

One of the most striking scenes in his life was his bold denunciation of the chieftain Coroticus, who, though calling himself a Christian, made a descent upon the Irish coast and murdered several of the natives, and carried off a number to sell as slaves. And the Churches which he and his companions founded were certainly lights in the darkness of that pagan country, which not only illuminated it, but became sources and centres of light to the whole of Western Europe.

What is known as his "Confession" is really a *confessio fidei*, the avowal of his faith, and a brief memoir of his life and work in Ireland. It bears strong resemblance, as a Creed, to the symbol of Nicea. It illustrates, after the manner of the Benedicite, the superstitious worship of nature which he attacked. Plainly recognizing the three orders of the Ministry, and with entire simplicity and freedom from any of the extravagant legends which we find in the lives which *other people* wrote *of* him (the earliest of which dates from the ninth century, and the most elaborate of which belongs to the thirteenth century), it gives us the story of an earnest and holy man, fearless and faithful in his nature, who well earned for himself in the best sense of the word, the title of the Apostle of Ireland. The probability is that he died on the 17th of March, A.D. 493. And his true glory consists in the fact that he was enabled, not to *found* the Church in Ireland because he found it there, nor to convert the whole people to Christianity; but to throw into the feeble current of its religious life, the strong warm tide of his own personal enthusiasm and his intense self-consecration; and so to spread and swell its wave of holy influence, and make the waste places of a pagan country, green—a very emerald isle—with the refreshing streams of Christian truth.

Of Columba we have, in the authenticated writings of Adamnan, a picture painted by his successor after an interval of about one hundred years. Columba was born in 521 at Gartan, in the County Donegal. The slab of stone on which his mother lay when the child was born is still shown, and one cannot fail to feel the picturesque pathos of certain legends connected with it. Himself a wanderer and traveller for more than thirty years of his life, and always with the intensest love and longing to return to his native land deep in his heart, yet this stone is said to hold a sovereign remedy against home-sickness; so much so, that to-day Irish emigrants flock to touch this stone, as they are leaving their old home for their new, remembering their great missionary. We know from Columba's life, and we know from very touching instances of the Irish emigrants of to-day, how little the long travelling and the wide parting sever the hearts of either from their first home.

The curious legend of the cause that gave rise to Columba's banishment is at least characteristic of the saint in two features: his love of learning, and his dominant, fiery, intense zeal. Angered first, the story goes, by the king's decision that he must return to the Abbot Finnian the stolen copy of the Psalter ("to every cow her calf;" to every book its copy), he was led further to carry out his threatened vengeance, when the king put to death a young prince of Connaught, who had taken refuge with Columba from being punished for an involuntary murder. He executed this vengeance by stirring up the chieftains of his own tribe and of the Connaught clans to a destructive war, in which the slaughter was enormous. When this fit of vengeance had passed over he was overwhelmed with remorse, alike by the accusations of his conscience, and by the judgment of his superiors, and set himself to do and bear a double penance: first, of exile from his beloved country; and next, of converting to Christianity a number of pagans equal to the number of Christians who had been slain in the battle. To this he consecrated his life with a reality and intenseness which, even when we have discarded the extravagant stories of his career, win for him a glorious title of honour in the roll of the greatest missionaries of the world.

He was forty-two years old when he set sail with twelve companions, in the year 563, in a frail wicker boat covered with hide, braving the stormy seas and dangerous coasts, and landed, we are told, first on the little island of Oronsay. Climbing a low hill near the shore, he found the coasts of Ireland still in sight; and, either because he did not dare to trust himself within view of his beloved country, or because he felt that he must entirely separate himself from it, he re-embarked and landed on the island of Iona. Anything more bleak and barren, "sullen" Montalembert calls it, than this little strip of treeless, flat earth, cannot be imagined. Rocky, sandy, unyielding, save by the most severe toil, of pasture for flocks or crops for men, and only about three miles and a half long by two miles wide, it became the centre of some of the widest-spread and most deeply-rooted missionary enterprises of the Christian world. No one who sets foot on it can fail to feel that Johnson's language, in the description of his tour to the Hebrides, is only too weak. "We were now treading," he says, "that illustrious island which was once the luminary of the Caledonian regions, whence savage clans and roving barbarians derived the benefit of knowledge and the blessing of religion." "That man is little to be envied whose patriotism would not be enforced upon the plain of Marathon, or whose piety would not grow warmer among the ruins of Iona." So William Croswell sang, in Auburn, fifty years ago:

> " The pilgrim at Iona's shrine
> Forgets his journey's toil,
> As faith rekindles in his breast
> On that inspiring soil."

To-day the halo of his wonderful name hangs over it like a spell. Only the very earth itself remains to tell the story of his life, his journeyings and his death. The tombs of the kings speak of its widespread fame of sanctity, which brought sovereigns of Norway and Spain, as well as British and Celtic kings, there for burial; Duncan among the rest whom Macbeth murdered, and who, Shakespeare says, "was carried to Colmes Kill, the sacred storehouse of his predecessors, and guardian of their bones." The ruins that remain of the ecclesiastical buildings are connected with another of the sacred and poetical characters of Scottish history, St. Margaret, whose beautiful and beloved memory not only lives in the old Abbey of Dunfermline, but is associated with St. Columba in the memories of the Scottish people; from the fact that in 1093 she built here the Chapel of St. Oran, whose walls still stand, the successor of the successive churches of Columba, built first of wattles, then of wood, which had to be brought to the island from the neighboring shore. The Cathedral, as it is called, though it must mark some holy site, and though its ruins have rung with the holy utterances of an ancient and uncorrupted faith, is of a date not earlier than the twelfth century. It is claimed that McLean's Cross, one of the two dignified crosses which have survived the barbarous prejudice of Christian men, is the cross which Adamnan names in his life of Columba, as associated with the spot where the saint rested on the last day of his life, and where the old white horse of the monastery came weeping to bid him farewell. But the spot where one is thrilled intensely with the magic power of this remarkable life, is the hill which he climbed that Saturday night with infinite difficulty, and where since then hosts of pilgrims have fulfilled his latest prophecy, delivered there, " To this spot, although small and mean, shall come not only kings and people of the Scots, but the rulers of barbarous and remote nations with their people." Passing from this place to the monastery, he could only half finish the verse of the Psalter he was copying, " They that seek the Lord shall want no manner of thing that is good," and on that Sunday morning, June the 9th, A.D. 597, having hastened, before the monks, to the matins of the festival, he died * before the Altar, among his spiritual children, who hurried to him in the dim light before the dawn, to get his last blessing. The voice was gone, and the power of the right hand to uplift itself. But raised by another, he made with it the sign of the cross, and passed, with a benediction in his heart, to receive the benediction of his Lord.

The heroism and enterprise of this man are among the mightiest records of missionary adventures for Christ that the world has known. Of fifty-three churches and monasteries which he founded, and which have left their traces in what is now called Scotland, thirty-two were in the Western Isles, and twenty-one in the northern country of Caledonia, which remained in the hands of the

* "Such was the life and death of the first great Apostle of Great Britain," says Montalembert. "We have lingered, perhaps too long, on the grand form of this monk, rising up before us from the mists of the Hebridean Sea, who, for the third part of a century, spread over those sterile isles and gloomy shores a pure and fertilizing light. In a confused age and unknown regions he displayed all that is the greatest and purest, and, it must be added, most easily forgotten in human genius: the gift of ruling souls by ruling himself. To select the most marked and graphic incidents from the general tissue of his life, and those most fit to unfold that which attracts the modern reader—that is, his personal character and influence upon contemporary events—from a world of minute details having almost exclusive reference to matters supernatural, has been no easy task.

savage Picts. They had lapsed after St. Ninian's death, into the violence of their ancestors; and when Columba virtually bearded their king in Inverness, he was at the mercy of their lawless ways, and exposed himself to the cruelty of the Druid priests. In spite of the dangers of the ocean travel, he was constantly in his boat, crossing and re-crossing the dangerous gulfs and bays, and going frequently back to Ireland, to begin or re-establish religious foundations. He shared in all the labors of the agriculture, and in the perils of the navigation, of his fellow monks; and it is no extravagance of language to say, that Iona began under him, and for two centuries continued, to be "the nursery of Bishops, the centre of education, the asylum of religious knowledge, the point of

But when this is done, it becomes comparatively easy to represent to ourselves the tall old man, with his fine and regular features, his sweet and powerful voice, the Irish tonsure high on his shaven head, and his long locks falling behind, clothed with his monastic cowl, and seated at the prow of his coracle, steering through the misty archipelagoes and narrow lakes of the north of Scotland, and bearing from isle to isle and from shore to shore, light, justice and truth, the life of the conscience and of the soul.

"He was at the same time full of contradictions and contrasts—at once tender and irritable, rude and courteous, ironical and compassionate, caressing and imperious, grateful and revengeful—led by pity as well as by wrath, ever moved by generous passions, and among all passions fired to the very end of his life by two, which his countrymen union among the British Isles, the capitol and necropolis of the Celtic race."

Alongside of the wider current of testimony which this whole history supplies against the recognition of any papal claim of supremacy, runs a tide of equally important witness, which has been strangely perverted. The organization of the monastic system for the missionary work of these early missionaries, and the absolute power of the abbots, have given rise to an argument for a Presbyterian system of government which is as unfounded as the legendary invention of Roman control. That the inherent and essential antagonism between monks and Bishops began from the first, may be taken for granted, since it is as much a proverb as that which grew out of it in the

understand the best, the love of poetry and the love of his country. Little inclined to melancholy when he had once surmounted the great sorrow of his life, which was his exile; little disposed even, save toward the end, to contemplation or solitude, but trained by prayer and austerities to triumphs of evangelical exposition ; despising rest, untiring in mental and manual toil, born for eloquence and gifted with a voice so penetrating and sonorous that it was thought of afterwards as one of the most miraculous gifts that he had received of God ; frank and loyal, original and powerful in his words as in his actions—in cloister and mission and parliament, on land or on sea, in Ireland as in Scotland; always swayed by the love of God and of his neighbor, whom it was his will and pleasure to serve with an impassioned uprightness—such was Columba. Besides the monk cathedrals of the old foundation, namely, the rivalry between Bishops and Deans. But nothing is clearer, in the whole ancient story, than the enormous multiplication of Bishops, the recognition of the Diocesan Episcopate, and the absolutely exclusive reservation of the right of conferring orders, to the Bishops. As to the number of Bishops, the story of St. Patrick's consecrations furnishes sufficient proof. The titles of the British Bishops present at Arles, Eborius of York, Restitutus of London, and Adelfius of Caerleon-on-Usk, prove that the historic Episcopacy was Diocesan. It remains to look at the matter of the monasteries, and the relation of Bishops to them. First of the monasteries themselves. † " The monastic character of the Church gave a peculiar stamp to her missionary work, which caused her to set about it in a mode well calculated to impress a people still to a great extent under the in-

and the missionary there was in him the making of a sailor, a soldier, poet, and orator. To us, looking back, he appears a personage as singular as he is lovable, in whom through all the mists of the past and all the cross-lights of legends, the man may still be recognized under the saint—a man capable and worthy of the supreme honor of holiness, since he knew how to subdue his inclinations, his weakness, his instincts, and his passions, and to transform them into docile and invincible weapons for the salvation of souls and the glory of God."—*Monks of the West.*

† Skene, Celtic Churches.

fluence of heathenism. It is difficult for us now to realize to ourselves what such pagan life really was —its hopeless corruption, its utter disregard of the sanctity of domestic ties, its injustice and selfishness, its violent and bloody character; and these characteristics would not be diminished in a people who had been partially Christianized, and had fallen back from it into heathenism. The monastic missionaries did not commence their work, as the earlier secular Church would have done, by arguing against their idolatry, superstition, and immorality, and preaching a purer faith; but they opposed to it the antagonistic characteristics and purer life of Christianity. They asked and obtained a settlement in some small and valueless island. There they settled down as a little Christian colony, living under a monastic rule requiring the abandonment of all that was attractive in life. They exhibited a life of purity, holiness and self-denial. They exercised charity and benevolence, and they forced the respect of the surrounding pagans to a life, the motives of which they could not comprehend, unless they resulted from principles higher than those their pagan religion afforded them; and having won their respect for their lives and their gratitude for their benevolence, these monastic missionaries went among them with the Word of God in their hands, and preached to them the doctrines and pure morality of the Word of Life."

As to the relation of the Episcopate to these monastic families, it is of course true that the Bishop, if a member of the monastery, was subject as such member to the rule and authority of the abbot: and very often in order to avoid the restraint of Episcopal authority each monastery had its own Bishop, sometimes as abbot, sometimes as a member of the family. Indeed it is said that Columba was only ordained Priest by mistake, it having been intended to make him Bishop. But of the recognition of the separate Order, alike in its duties and its dignities, there can be no question. Orders were always conferred by the Bishops and *only* by them. When the Bishop officiated as celebrant he broke the Bread, alone. And Adamnan records the fact, that on one occasion, when a Bishop came to the monastery at Iona not avowing his rank, St. Columba was greatly distressed, because in the ignorance of his office, the respect due to it had not been paid him.

There is a link to be inserted here, both in order that one may save the appearance of too wide a gap in the sequence of the story, and in order to assure the connection between the Celtic missionaries and the Church of England of to-day. There are good and sufficient reasons why we have less distinct detail of the story of Christianity in central and southern England, than in

Cornwall or Ireland or Wales; because, as by the ravages of fire and flood, populations were wiped out of existence or banished to remoter regions of safety. But that it certainly *was there*, with Churches, congregations, Dioceses and Bishops, down to the time when the Roman legions were withdrawn from Britain, is undoubted. The names of the Sees and the Bishops that filled them are left; and we have the relic of a treatise on the Christian life written by Fastidius, who was Bishop, probably of London, at this time. The founding of these Churches can be traced to no other, than the same source from which Christianity found its way to the other portions of Britain After this time, desolated by the Picts and Scots, depleted by famine, and devastated by civil wars among the native chiefs, Churton's statement is undoubtedly true, that "from the year 449," when the Saxons were invited by the Britons to protect them from the Picts and Scots, "Christianity began to disappear from the most important and fruitful provinces of Britain. As the Saxons founded one after another of their petty kingdoms, they destroyed the Churches, and the Priests fled before them. Some found refuge in the colony of Brittany, and others escaped to the borders of Wales." "There were British Bishops still dwelling in the invaded parts, as long as there were any means of assembling a flock of Christians around them;" and "no doubt," "it was so appointed by God's Providence, that Christianity should be planted in North Britain, at the very time when it was nearly driven out at the south, that the means of its restoration might be at hand." The fact is that the story of St. Alban really belongs here as evidence of the early and earnest existence of Christianity in this part of England, for the scene of his life and death was at the town of Verulam, close to the site of the present Abbey Church which bears his name.

His name is best authenticated in the history of the early Church in England, as given by Bede, whose account is based partly upon legend and partly upon the history of Gildas. It has at least these well attested facts:

His martyrdom occurred during the persecution of Diocletian. Himself a pagan, he had received into his house a Priest flying from his persecutors, and was so impressed by the faith and holiness of the man, that after instruction he embraced the Christian faith. When the soldiers of the governor came to his house, instead of surrendering the guest whom they sought, he put on his long cloak and was led, bound, before the judge. No entreaty or violence could induce him to surrender his faith, and he was finally taken to the bank of a river and put to death. The miracle of the receding water, and the uprising of the living spring, and the conversion of the executioner are well known, and it is curious to notice that in the twelfth-century version of his story the long cloak or amphibalus, in which the martyr was clad, is transformed into the name of the priest in whose stead he suffered, and becomes St. Amphibalus, who is said to have been martyred later on. It is notable also, not only that the first British martyr whose name comes down to us was a layman, as the first martyr of the Christian Church in early times was a Deacon; but that his name, suggesting the white robe of the saints, is preserved both in the earlier name of a portion of Scotland, and also in the title of a duke belonging to the Royal House of England; and I am glad to say, through him, in the Capital City of this great State (as part of its historic relation to colonial days), and in the Diocese whose Bishop I am privileged to be.

St. Ninian's mission to the southern Picts is an instance of the way in which the tide of Christian teaching ebbed to and fro; for he went from Cumbria, of whose British King he is said to have been the son, to Galloway, a *British* missionary of the *British* Church.

When Augustine landed, there can be no question but that, owing to the circumstances which have been just mentioned, Christianity in southern England was the shadow of a name. And when after his death, and the death of Ethelbert, the progress of that mission was rudely arrested, so that nothing was left of it except in Kent; when Paulinus, who had labored for the conversion of the Northumbrians, returned to Rochester; the providential protection of the old centres of light among the Celts fulfilled its gracious purpose. St. Aidan, assisted by a band of Columban missionaries, succeeded in restoring Christianity among the Northumbrians, abundantly aided by Oswald the king, who had himself in early youth found refuge in Iona, and been there taught Christianity and baptized. Attended by the king himself, who acted as interpreter to the Irish missionaries, Aidan, wandering on foot, preached to the peasants of Yorkshire and Northumbria. And as Oswald gradually extended his dominion until he was once called "Emperor of the whole of Britain," the supremacy of the Cross was asserted. After Oswald's death, a tide of heathenism swept back again, but it was not for long. And after the death of Penda, Central England was won back to the religion of Christ, by what Green calls, "a victory for Irish Christianity." St. Aidan, St. Chad and St. Cuthbert are the three names, all children and descendants really of Columba, most closely associated with the British Christianity which makes the link in that age, between the Celtic Churches and the Church of England of to-day.

But it will be noticed, meanwhile, that the native Church which resisted Augustine's claim to foreign jurisdiction, was represented in the conference on the banks of the Severn by nine Bishops, seven of whom came from Wales, and two from Somerset and Cornwall. "We are bound," the Bishops said, "to serve the Church of God, and the Bishop of Rome, and every godly Christian as far as helping them in offices of love and charity. This service we are ready to pay, but more than this we do not know to be due to him, or to any other. We have a primate of our own who is to oversee us for God, and to keep us in the way of spiritual life."

I pass over, not thoughtlessly or with indifference to all we secured out of it, the story of Augustine's mission to England. There can be no question but that the efforts which the British Church had made to convert the invaders of Britain had failed. The religion of central and southern England at the end of the sixth century was as pagan as when they first landed. The old story, favorite and familiar as it is, of the strong purpose of Gregory the Great, formed when he was Abbot of the Celian Monastery, and carried out after he became Bishop of Rome, hardly needs repetition. The Angles, who were angels coming from the Province of Deira, to be rescued "*de ira Dei*," that so their king, named

Ella, might sing Alleluia, was one of those plays on words of which the monks were very fond, and which led to the very noble work of Augustine's mission.

Sometimes I think that Augustine's real greatness has been merged in our admiration for the great Pope. Really, the courage with which he pursued his journey in spite of all alarms and threats, the dignity with which they presented themselves before King Ethelbert, chanting their litany to the Gregorian tones, and then the quiet way in which they settled down to their half monastic and half missionary life add great picturesqueness to the story, as they gave great power to the effect of their work. Bertha, the Queen, was already a Christian, and it was to the little Church where her own Priest celebrated the offices of religion, that Augustine and his followers went for their worship.

On Whitsunday, 597, the King was baptized, and on the following Christmas day it is said that ten thousand English converts received the holy sacrament of Baptism. Augustine brought with him, undoubtedly, the belief which was growing more and more on the Italian Church in his time, that all Bishops and Churches owed allegiance to the See of Rome; and he found steady and stern resistance on the part of all the British Bishops and Christians to this claim, or to any demand that he should be recognized as set over them. That resistance lasted on and on, involving questions not merely of the keeping of Easter, but of the method of Baptism, and the whole matter of jurisdiction. And while in obedience to Gregory's large-minded instructions, as to the introduction of the Gallican use, Augustine yielded in regard to the liturgies, he remained firm in his claim of jurisdiction over the British Churches; and the result, due partly to insular independence, partly to national pride, partly to ecclesiastical conviction and, through all, to the Providence of God, was a schism between the British and the English Churches.

It is a wonderful fact, that when, owing to the relapse into paganism of Ethelbert's son when he came to the throne, and to a similar reaction among the eastern Saxons, all that Augustine had gained was lost after his death, except in the kingdom of Kent, it was reserved to St. Aidan, the successor of Columba, assisted by a band of missionaries from Iona, to refresh and restore what Augustine had begun. His See was fixed in Lindisfarn, called afterward the Holy Island; and from that time on there was a gradual eating away of the national independence of the British Church, until in the eleventh century, very largely under the influence of Queen Margaret, the subjection was virtually completed.

But two things not only deserve but demand our attention. First, that England has had more Christian centuries of independence than of subordination. And secondly, that although sent as a monk by Gregory, and receiving afterwards from him the pallium which declared his own personal allegiance, Augustine's orders as Bishop came from Etherius, the Bishop of Arles, and so were Gallican and Eastern, through Polycarp and St. John.

I have no time, no right, no need to speak of these four centuries which belong to the next lecture in this course. But as it is part of the story of Iona and the Celtic Church to tell of Oswald the King, and Aidan the Bishop, so it is still the story of Columba and Iona, to speak of Margaret the Queen. And really among all the figures that pass before us in this panoramic review of the early story of Christian work in Britain, certainly none is more beautiful and attractive than hers. "Mirror of wives, mothers and queens," and mother of many kings, her character is most remarkable in its combination of all that we call manly in courage and strength of intellect and purpose, and of all we know to be womanly in tenderness, purity, gentleness and devotion. Of course, one recognizes always with pain and regret, that it was largely due to her strong influence, that the second "Roman occupation of Britain" was brought about, seven centuries after pagan Rome had left it; but no prejudice can blind our eyes to the influence of her holy character and the beauty of her saintly life.

We have an authenticated account of her in the memoir written by Turgot, who was her confessor and intimate friend, Prior of Durham and Bishop of St. Andrews, and who died in 1115. He calls himself in the prologue of the life "a servant of the servants of St. Cuthbert."

She was the granddaughter of King Edmund, who was known for his matchless valor as "Edmund the Ironside." Her coming to Scotland was brought about by the wars and massacres attending the past struggles of the Saxons against the Normans. At the death of Harold, Edgar, the brother of Margaret, though still a boy, was chosen King; and after the defeat of the English, he fled with his mother and his two sisters to seek shelter at the court of Malcolm, King of Scotland, who received them at Dunfermline and persuaded Margaret to give up her purpose of becoming a nun and to marry him.

Mr. Freeman says of this marriage that it was "through Margaret that the old kingly blood of England passed into the veins of the descendants of the Conqueror. The tree runs back to the root when Henry the First marries Matilda, the daughter of Margaret, and it bears leaves at the birth of her children." And we must remember how distinguished the royal line was that descended from her in the kings Edgar, Alexander and David and their descendants; so that Scotland for two hundred years was governed by seven admirable kings, all tracing their life and character to her.

Turgot's description of the personal relations between Margaret and Malcolm is very touching and interesting. He was an unlettered savage really, whom she refined and elevated and Christianized; and although he could not read, he would turn over and examine books which she used either for her devotion or her study; and whenever he heard her express especial liking for a particular book, he would look at it with special interest, kissing it, and often taking it into his hands. Sometimes he sent for a worker in precious metals, whom he commanded to ornament that volume with gold and gems; and when the work was finished, the king himself used to carry the book to the queen, as a loving proof of his devotion. She had a strong sense of the dignity of royalty, and kept up the kingly estate with great precision and care; but through all, her own heart was fixed upon higher and holier things. She lived really a life of religious meditation and perpetual consecration to God. And her great anxiety and care, and the exercise both of her authority and her influence, in reforming various corruptions in the Church of Scotland at that time, make her truly one of the "nursing mothers" of the Church. As to the observance of Lent and the offering of the Holy Eucharist, the keeping of the Lord's Day and the matter of lawful as against unlawful marriages, she counselled with the clergy and by her own example, influence and authority reformed many things that had gone wrong.

Her charities were unbounded; so much so that Turgot says that she was poorer than any of her paupers, often stripping herself and her attendants of garments that they had on, to give to those who were in want, that none should go away in distress. "Now and then," Turgot says, "she helped herself to something or other out of the king's private property, it mattered not what it was, to give to a poor person; and this pious plundering the king always took pleasantly and in good part. It was his custom to offer certain coins of gold upon Maundy Thursday and at High Mass, some of which coins the queen often devoutly pillaged and bestowed on the beggar who was petitioning her for help. Although the king was fully aware of the theft, he generally pretended to know nothing of it, and felt much amused by it. Now and then he caught the queen in the very act, with the money in her hand, and laughingly threatened that he would have her arrested, tried, and found guilty."

This whole story of Queen Margaret is surrounded, as almost all these histories are, with the atmosphere of marvels through which it is difficult to see the real truth of history; but there can be no question of the beauty and holiness of her life, of the wonderful influence that she had over her husband, and of the moral value of her reforms in the Church; over and against which is to be set the fact that it was through her influence that the last resistance to the intrusion of the Bishop of Rome was overcome, and that for a little while England became Roman again.

It is with her that the story of the Holy Rood is connected, in honour of which the youngest of her sons, King David, built a Church; and it was with this sacred relic in her hand that she died, just at the moment that her son Edgar brought news that Malcolm had been slain in battle. Although the ruins of Dunfermline no longer guard the actual tomb of the saint, they speak of her beautiful memory all the more eloquently, because of the contrast with the ugly reminder of puritan Scotland which has been built on to it. And the place where she was buried, recently restored by the carefulness of Queen Victoria, is a shrine to which many reverent and loving people make frequent pilgrimages.

Her biographer stops in the middle of the recital of a wonderful story of the preservation, after its immersion in water, of her book of the Gospels, to say what we may all endorse, " I leave it to others to admire the tokens of miracles which they see elsewhere. I admire much more the works of mercy which I perceived in Margaret, for signs are common to the good and the bad, whereas works of piety and true charity belong to the good only. The former sometimes are the proof of holiness, the latter are that which constitutes it."

My reverend brother who is to take up the story of the Anglo-Saxon Church will not feel that I have trenched upon his portion of the history, if I recall, merely to pass over it the simple fact that the *Gregorian tone* which entered, through St. Augustine, into the worship of the ancient Celtic Church, was a "*tonus peregrinus*": not "the Lord's song in a strange land," but a strange song, in a land that was already the Lord's. Like bells jangled out of tune, it was the source of a discord which jars upon the ear, for centuries.

My one concern with it is to call your attention to the fact, that the Roman mission was, and is, and always will be exotic in England; and that it really had no strong or permanent hold in England. At the end of the seventh century the whole of England was in communion with the Scoto-Celtic Church except Kent, East Anglia, Wessex and Sussex; and of these exceptions Sussex was heathen, Wessex was under a Bishop in Gallican Orders, and in communion with the British Bishops, so that Kent and East Anglia alone remained in subjection to Canterbury and Rome. In central England, Christianity was really extinct at the close of the fifth century by the massacre of Christians and the removal of the survivors to the north. The Britons in North Wales remained independent of Rome until the end of the eighth century; in Cornwall till the middle of the tenth; in southern England and Ireland till the beginning of the eighth; in Scotland till the middle of the eleventh century, and Ireland did not entirely surrender until nearly the middle of the twelfth; so that the Roman occupation of Britain ecclesiastically was really only for these four centuries, from the twelfth to the sixteenth, about equal to the duration of the civil dominion of Rome in the first centuries.

And such was the energy of the Celtic missionary monks that between the fifth and eighth centuries they had entered Gaul, Italy, Switzerland and Germany; and even reached the Faroe Isles and Iceland; so that the Celtic Church extended from Iceland to Spain, from the Atlantic to the Danube, from Ireland to Italy.

Is there, the question recurs, any living relation between the Church of England to-day and the old founding among the Celts and Britons? I think there is. The remains of the earlier liturgies are few; but certain distinctive and characteristic features of Celtic Christianity are very marked, as showing in them the influence of the Galatian and Mozarabic Liturgies; and as reproduced in our own. Of the latter may be instanced the biddings to prayer, called prefaces; which have a resemblance at least to our exhortations; the place of the commemoration of the departed *after* the Offertory, rather than as in the Roman use after, and as part of, the Consecration Prayer; the use of a hymn after the consecration in the Communion Office; the administration of the Holy Communion in both kinds; the use of confession to a Priest left optional (in the Celtic Church it seems to have been public); and the observance of the Rogation days, unknown in the Roman Church until the time of Leo Third. Of the former, we find very marked features of a Gallican and Mozarabic character, as for instance the singing of the hymn Benedicite, before the Epistle or the Gospel; the use of several, sometimes seven collects instead of the one; the Lection from the Old Testament beside the Epistle and Gospel; the Episcopal benediction given after the consecration and fraction of the Bread; reservation *in both kinds* for the sick, and the use of unleavened bread.

A very curious and striking instance is found also in the rule that, in the Holy Eucharist, if the celebrant were a Bishop he consecrated alone, if a

Priest he had a Priest associated with him; whereas in the Roman use the Bishop always had a Priest associated with him who joined in the words of consecration. It was this habit which furnished an instance of the respect that Columba paid to the Episcopal office, for once, Adamnan records, a stranger from the Province of Munster who concealed through humility the fact that he was a Bishop, was invited on the next Sunday by Columba to join with him in consecrating the Body of Christ, that as Priests they might break the Bread of the Lord together. Columba on going to the Altar discovered his rank and addressed him thus: "Christ bless thee, brother: consecrate alone as a Bishop, now that we know that thou art of that rank. Why hast thou endeavored to disguise this, and so prevent us giving thee the honour due to thee?"

More than this, I think there is a likeness, which proves a lineal descent, between the Church of England of the last three centuries and the Celtic Church of the older days. Something else beside Wicklif's ashes was carried by the Severn to the sea. The spirit of the nine British Bishops who, on the bank of the Severn, under what was called St. Augustine's Oak, held their conference with the great Gregory's great missionary—that spirit of the old British Bishops revived and lived again in Cranmer and Ridley and Latimer. The heart of the oak was British; and only sheltered Augustine for a time. Its root was in its native soil. And from the Severn to the sea, and over the seas to us, and over *all* seas, as the Church of England goes with English commerce and English colonization to the ends of the earth, it is the old life, autonomous, independent, needing and knowing no fountain-head but Christ, and charged alike with the spirit and the power, the privilege and the responsibility, of bearing the sound of the Gospel into all lands, and its words unto the ends of the world.

There is a yew tree in the churchyard at Crowhurst in Surrey, which bears the botanical marks, allowed by scientific experts, of fifteen hundred years of life: so that it might have heard the victorious shouts of the battle of the Hallelujah, and listened to St. Germanus, refreshing with a new current of Catholic truth the old Galatian heritage of British Christianity. It is in a churchyard; and it suits some people to deal with it therefore as a memorial of mourning and a suggestion of decay. Shall it not rather tell us how, in God's acre, it stands to preach the blessed story of "mortality swallowed up in life," of the old deeply-rooted tree of primitive Christianity, which draws its very nourishment from the decay of the generations that it shelters and survives; which graces and guards the graves of successive and continuous

Christian centuries; which witnesses, with every wind that waves its spreading branches, to its "rooting and grounding" in eternal truth? The emblematic, ever-green yew tree is the symbol of the imperishableness of the British Church, green in its old age; which has fulfilled the hope, that passes still into our prayers, *Floreat radix.* "She stretches forth her branches unto the sea, and her boughs unto the river." "The hills are covered with the shadow of it; and the boughs thereof are like the goodly cedar trees." God made room for it, and "when it had taken root it filled the land."

The Anglo-Saxon Church.

LECTURE II.

THE REV. SAMUEL HART, D.D.,
Professor of Latin at Trinity College, Hartford.

THE ANGLO-SAXON CHURCH.

THE history of the Anglo-Saxon Church is the history of the Church of the English people, during the first centuries of their life in the home which they had conquered for themselves in the island of Britain. The former inhabitants of that island, who were dispossessed by these invaders from the continent, had indeed been converted to Christianity; they formed a part of that Celtic Church, the history of which has been lately presented to you. But the Angles and Saxons and Jutes were heathens when they crossed the sea in the fifth and sixth centuries, and they were in no way affected by the political organizations, the social customs, or the religious faith of those whom they swept before them into the mountains of Wales and the peninsula of Cornwall. The British Christians, not without brave attempts at resistance, fell back before the ruthlessly cruel invaders; and nearly the whole of what we now call England—the country south of the Tweed and east of the Dee and the Severn—became again an utterly heathen land. In the long strife the worshippers of Woden and of Thor had overcome and expelled the worshippers of Christ; in the conquered land there were none left to tell the conquerors the story of His truth, nor did the British Christians venture from their hiding-places to teach it to the savages of whom they had good reason to stand in dread.

The story of the conversion of the English—for such we may fairly call them after the time when they had taken possession of the land in which their descendants dwell to-day—is a story of wonderful and romantic interest. And that interest is by no means confined to the time of the conversion of the people to Christianity. The whole period during which the English Church was laying its foundations and beginning the erection of that stately fabric which was destined to be the mother-city of Churches beyond the seas and a firm bulwark of the truth in times of its utmost danger — the whole of the Anglo-Saxon period is filled with events which call forth all the enthusiasm of faith, and its history is crowded with the names of great men. We find pervading it a touching simplicity, as we read of the words and deeds of bishops and of kings, who with all of a father's love cared for both the temporal and the eternal interests of their children in the Church and in the State; a faithful, unquestioning obedience to the Christ Whom they preached, and to Whom they had devoted their lives, corresponding to which we are scarce surprised to read the record of what would be in our days extraordinary manifestations of Divine approval and help; and withal an earnest determination to impart to others the truth and the blessings which were worth so much to themselves. Outside of the limits of the great world-empire, which still in name asserted the power and the prerogatives of the Caesars, outside of the lands in which the language of that empire was the speech of civilized men, there grew up during some five centuries the one purely national Church of the West. Influenced by Rome so far as to be brought into touch with the life of the great Catholic Church, independent of Rome so far as to assert and maintain the rights of a national Church as they were then understood, our English ancestors of that early day were beginning a work, the importance of which was quite beyond the reach of their imagination. The conversion of the English, the establishment of the English Church, the growth of a Christian English nation, form a chapter in history so full of records of apostolic faith and of primitive zeal and of practical applications of the law of Christianity, that it is hard to remember that, when we begin to read it, we are close at the opening of the seventh century of our era; it seems rather to belong to those earlier days when the virtues of Christian men were of that simple kind which best embodies the spirit of our religion, and when even their faults were such as pertain rather to the infirmities than to the vices of human nature.

I venture to think, gentlemen of the Church Club, that I can best remind you of the important facts in the history of the early English Church and of the work which it accomplished for its own time and for the future, by asking you to look at a few of the prominent scenes in that history. In nearly every case we shall find a famous man whose name is closely associated with a famous place.

I.

And first of all, we think of St. Augustine and of Canterbury; for with him and there the work of the Christianization of the English people began. Kent was not the most important of the kingdoms which the invaders had founded; but it was the place where the earliest permanent Teutonic settlement had been made: and it was not very closely connected with the other kingdoms; for its people were Jutes, while those of the others were Saxons or Angles; but it occupied the part of the island which was nearest the continent, and it was almost of necessity the place to which missionaries would first come. We all know the story of the pious monk Gregory, who, struck by the beauty of some fair-skinned and golden-haired youths whom he saw exposed in the slave-market at Rome, asked of what nation they were: when he was told that they were Angles, he said that they should rather be called angels; when he learned that they were from the province of Deira, he affirmed that they ought to be delivered from the ire of God; and still further, learning that the name of their king was Aella, declared that their tongues should be taught to sing Alleluia. But he did not content himself with playing upon words. His heart was touched, and he prayed, and obtained consent, that he might go to the end of the earth and preach the Gospel to the Angles. But this purpose could not be accomplished at once; and after a few years his election to the bishopric of Rome made it impossible for him to fulfil in person the plan which he had formed. Yet he did not forget the bright faces of the lads who had been brought from Yorkshire, very possibly having been captured by the men of Kent, to be sold as slaves at Rome; and soon he selected Augustine, the provost of his own monastery of St. Andrew, to lead a band of missionaries to the English. Perhaps, for reasons already suggested, he would under any circumstances have sent them at first to the southeastern peninsula; but he can hardly have been ignorant of the fact that there was at least the possibility of a more favorable opening there than elsewhere in the island. Ethelbert had been for thirty years king of Kent, and he had married Bertha, the daughter of a Frankish king, promising that she should be allowed the practice of her religion as a Christian, her chaplain being the Frankish bishop Liudhard.

It was after Easter in the year 597 that the missionaries landed on the isle of Thanet; and in the Ascension week, by permission of the king, they came to Canterbury. Outside the city stood the little church of St. Martin's, where St. Martin's Church stands to-day, the Roman brick in its walls still testifying to the great antiquity of a part at least of its structure, once the worshipping-place of a Christian congregation, then the chapel of a Christian queen. As they entered, Augustine, lifting up the Cross, took possession of Canterbury and of England for Christ. Then he and his brethren, chanting the Rogation antiphon which they had learned in Gaul, and adding to it the Gregorian Alleluia of the Easter-tide, prophesied of the struggle and the victory which lay before them, and with prayers and thanksgiving began their work. It was, we are told, the simplicity and purity and devotion of the lives of these men, which drew to them the hearts of the heathen among whom they had come to dwell. Soon Ethelbert himself was baptized, and soon Kent could be called a Christian kingdom ; and the conversion of Teutonic England began just as Columba, the great missionary of Celtic Britain, was breathing his last. Presently Augustine, at Gregory's direction, repaired to Arles in Gaul to receive consecration as a bishop ; and on his return, he restored an ancient Roman church within the walls of Canterbury, dedicated it to the Lord Christ, and made it his cathedral, while for those who had come with him he founded a monastery hard by. The stately pile which is the metropolitical church of all England is the Christ Church of Augustine's foundation, and the missionary college which bears his own name has rescued from desecration the site of the buildings that served to shelter the simple monks who first taught to the men of Kent the way of salvation.

Gregory the Great was a man of no meagre plans or narrow hopes. It was he, we are told, who first spoke of the people of England as if they were all one nation ; he authorized Augustine to use the powers of a metropolitan, consecrating twelve suffragans for himself ; and he planned that Deira, the land of the beautiful youths, further north, should also, when its people should become Christians, have a metropolitan with twelve suffragans. The plan was never carried into effect in all its details; fortunately for England, the arrangement of English dioceses followed the lines of the divisions and sub-divisions of English kingdoms, and was not guided by schemes drawn up at Rome and based on former Roman arrangements in Britain; it was a natural growth, not an artificial structure. But after all it was Gregory who planned the organization of all England into the form of a national Church.

And Gregory had plans also which included the Christians in the remoter part of the land to the heathen portion of which he had sent his missionaries. Writing to Augustine in reply to questions which he had addressed him as to certain matters, among them his relations to the British bishops, he had told him that he was to ask them to work with him in converting the Saxons, but had added, with a truly Roman assumption, that he was to consider them all as subject to the authority which he had established at Canterbury. Augustine thereupon asked the British bishops to meet him in conference; they came a first and a second time; they argued with him as to the three points of divergence between the Roman and the British Churches—the Easter rule and cycle, the shape of the tonsure, the ceremonies accompanying baptism; they were offended at what they thought to be an indication of arrogance on his part; they refused to yield to his demands and to unite with him in preaching to the Saxons; and Augustine returned to Kent unsuccessful and disappointed. Nearer home, however, his work made progress; Justus was consecrated bishop of Rochester, apparently the chief city of a petty kingdom of West Kent; and the king of the East Saxons, Ethelbert's nephew and dependent, became a Christian, and Mellitus was made first bishop of London.

Such is in outline what St. Augustine of Canterbury had accomplished, when, in the prospect of immediate death, he designated and consecrated his friend Laurence to be his successor, eight years after he had set foot on English soil. It is true that Augustine was not a great man, nor was he always a wise man; but he laid the foundations of a great work which was guided by a wisdom superior to his own. There have been those who have exaggerated his labors and their results, as if from him alone came the knowledge of Christianity to the British Isles; and there have been others who have looked upon his mission as almost a failure. The true estimate of what he did lies between the two. We cannot forget the British Christians, who kept the knowledge of the truth in the wild mountains of the west; we can not forget the debt which the north and the mid lands owed to the Celtic missionaries from the island of the saints; we must acknowledge that when Augustine died, his influence had not extended far: but he had brought Christianity to the English people; he had established a see, the power of which would soon be felt over a united nation and would at last extend throughout the world; and he had inspired into the English somewhat of the missionary zeal which already marked the Scots. Though he lived to consecrate but two of the proposed suffragans of his see, the result of his labors was soon felt outside of Kent and Essex. Along ways which he had pointed out, Felix of Burgundy was sent by one of his successors to East Anglia, and Birinus of Italy carried the Gospel to Wessex. And under more happy circumstances and in a more natural way than had marked his unsuccessful attempts, the remnant of the ancient British Church and the Celtic Church of the north were brought into union with the Roman mission, and the Church of the British isles was made one.

II.

The next scene which attracts our attention as marking a turning-point in the history is the council or conference at Whitby in the spring of the year 664; and the man who stands out prominently before us is the bishop Wilfrid. Before this time—and it was less than sixty years after Augustine's death—great changes had taken place. Ethelbert's son and successor had for a time refused Christianity, and Kent had nearly relapsed into paganism; but Ethelbert's sister had married Edwin of Northumbria, and she had taken with her to the northern kingdom Paulinus, who had been first consecrated a bishop. Edwin was converted, and, by a decision of his Witan, Northumbria became Christian; and Paulinus was recognized as bishop of York, including under his jurisdiction the land of Deira and extending his labors to Lincoln. But the north Welsh, joining themselves to the still heathen Mercians, invaded Northumbria; Edwin was killed, and Paulinus fled. Then Oswald, Edwin's nephew, took the throne, repulsed the Welsh, and while he extended his supremacy took care also to restore the Christian religion, to which he was devoutly attached. To accomplish this, he needed a bishop; and he sent to the far-off isle of Hy, the Iona of later days, the great centre of light and learning, the very name of which fills us even now with deep emotion. So Aidan came, consecrated by the Celtic bishops of Hy and bringing with him their customs, so strange in the eyes of those who were in the habit of looking to Rome as their pattern; and, with a love for an island home and a Celtic bishop's desire for retirement, he placed his bishop-stool on Lindisfarne, the holy island of the eastern coast. Aidan and Oswald labored and almost lived together until the still youthful king fell in battle slain by the heathen against whom he was defending the homes of his people; and soon Aidan was succeeded by Finan, another bishop from Hy. Under Finan the paschal question was raised, or at least revived, in Northumbria. The Scottish bishop followed the British use, claiming that it came from Ephesus and St. John; those who had received their Christianity from Kent or from Gaul followed the Roman use, basing it on the authority of St. Peter as the chief of the Apostles. The question was not the ancient quartodeciman controversy, of which we read in ante-Nicene times, though it was and is often confused with it; for both parties kept Easter on Sunday: it related partly to the cycle which should be used in determining the time of the ecclesiastical full moon, the British Christians not having learned of the tables adopted at Rome since they had ceased to have regular intercourse with that city, and partly (and especially) to the determination of the earliest day on which Easter might fall, the British keeping it on the day of the full moon if that fell on a Sunday, while the Romans in that case deferred it to the Sunday following. Each party accused the other of un-catholic action and of heresy; and the controversy was most persistent and bitter. Northumbria and Kent were not far apart, and had constant communication with each other; the two branches of the Church represented in these kingdoms were in many ways brought closely together; and it was impossible that a matter which both considered so important should be left undecided. In fact, the matter came still nearer home to the southern Christians; for Cedd, who had labored successfully among the East Saxons, had been consecrated by Finan and two other Scottish bishops to preside over the Church in that kingdom. Soon came the conflict between Colman, Finan's successor, himself of Scottish ordination, and Wilfrid. This Wilfrid was a Northumbrian of noble birth, who had visited Rome and Lyons, and had formed a strong attachment to the Roman see. He came back to take up his home at Ripon, and to feel and resent the peculiarities and the defects of the Christianity which had been brought to his native land from the uncouth Christians of the north. He was determined that the civilized customs should not yield to those which were barbarous, and that the Roman should displace the Celtic Easter.

A conference was called, which, as has been said, met in the year 664, at Whitby, on a lofty bluff overlooking the northern sea, lately chosen as the site of a monastery. In arguing the case, Colman appealed to the ancient custom of his Church; Wilfrid urged the extended influence of the Roman Church and the power which the Lord had given to St. Peter. The king decided, solely (as it would seem) from the latter argument, that Rome must be right; and Colman withdrew to the western isles. The controversy had been about a matter of very little importance, save as it affected uniformity of usage and brotherly charity; and we are inclined to regret here, as so often in later history, the stamping out of local usage by the harsh assumptions of the Roman see. Yet, so far as there was a right and a wrong in this matter, Rome was in the right; and the conference of Whitby kept the English Church from becoming isolated from the living and growing Christianity which was gaining so much and so useful power in western Europe. Had the matter been decided otherwise, English Christianity could hardly have escaped disruption, and it would at least have been cramped in a narrow mould and so prevented from accomplishing the work which lay before it. We cannot but sympathize with the Celtic bishop who went back sorrowfully to his former home; but we can see that Wilfrid saved the English Church from the danger of becoming a tribal and monastic Church and from falling into that Irish chaos which overwhelmed all order and discipline. At Whitby a most important step was taken, while yet there was in no strict sense a nation of the English, towards establishing a national English Church.

It would be instructive and interesting, had we the time, to trace out in some detail the after life of Wilfred; but a few words must suffice for such facts as bear upon the progress of the history. He was soon chosen bishop of York; and, unwilling to accept consecration from those whom he called schismatics, he went to France and was consecrated by the bishop of Paris. But he was long in returning; and when he came to Northumbria, he found that Chad had been consecrated in his place by Wina of Wessex and two bishops from West Wales—the first step towards an actual union of the English Church with the Welsh, but the last time for centuries that any English bishop had a consecrator outside of the Roman communion. Wilfrid retired and worked faithfully in Mercia and Kent, until he was restored to York. There, after a time of much labor and great success, he incurred the displeasure of the king and placed himself in opposition to the plans of Archbishop Theodore (of whom we shall hear presently); and when a part of his diocese was removed from his jurisdiction without his consent, he determined to carry an appeal in person to Rome. On his way his ship landed him in Friesland; there his love of adventure and of work prevailed for a time, and he became the first English missionary, moving the hearts of the rude people to hear and to accept the truth. At last he went to Rome; his case was heard by a council and determined in his favor; but now, as formerly when he went to France, he could not easily tear himself away from Rome. When he did reach Northumbria he produced the papal bull, only to discover that his appeal was regarded as disloyalty and that he was charged with having gained his case dishonestly. After imprisonment he was practically banished, and he found no resting-place till he came to Sussex, the only part of England that was still heathen. Here his missionary enthusiasm was again aroused; he first taught the barbarous people to catch fish, and then preached to them the Gospel; and for five years he stayed among them apparently without a murmur. Then Theodore sent him back again to the north, where once more he got into trouble, and whence once more he carried an appeal to Rome, to meet with success there, but to find that the papal decrees were not considered infallible in England. Wilfrid was now an old man; he consented to a compromise, and accepted Hexham and Ripon as his diocese for the rest of his life. The moral of his career is to be read all through English history. He succeeded when and where he identified himself with the people; but he could not easily identify himself with others than those who were willing to submit themselves to him. He failed when he ceased to act as an Englishman, to respect English prejudices, and to follow English customs; he failed when he appealed for justice to a foreign ruler, even to one whose authority in matters spiritual was highly respected; he failed when he attempted, though probably without intending it, to make the English Church a dependency of the Roman see. His virtues were those of the Englishman; his faults were those of the Roman.

III.

But we must pass now, stepping a little back in the history, to the important, though little known, Council of Hertford, and to the great man who presided at it, Theodore, called of Tarsus, archbishop of Canterbury. The place is north of London, not far from the spot where St. Albans points to the site of an ancient Roman city and preserves the memory of a tradition of British Christianity, and where a noble cathedral is crowned with a tower made largely of the Roman brick of Verulamium. The man who summoned an assembly of the English Church to meet there in 673, was one who united in himself the training of the East, a mission from the great imperial city, and the duties of a primacy in the far West. Theodore of Tarsus, Archbishop of Canterbury! We are reminded of the great apostle, whose birth and early training had been in the wealthy and learned city on the banks of the Cydnus, and who had carried the words of the Gospel past Rome to the very bounds of the West. So this scholar, taught in the secular learning of the schools of his native city and in the theology of the Oriental Church, having the tonsure of an eastern monk, already beyond what men call the prime of life, had come to Rome at a time when the English Church was in a weakened state, when a priest sent to Rome to be consecrated to the vacant see of Canterbury had died there, and when Hadrian, a Roman abbot to whom the position was offered, had declined to accept it. On Hadrian's recommendation, Theodore, not yet even a subdeacon, was designated for the post. He was obliged to tarry at Rome till his hair should be grown, that he might receive the Roman tonsure; and then, having been ordained and consecrated by the Pope himself, he set out on his journey to Britain, accompanied by Hadrian with instructions to see that he did not follow the Greeks in anything that was contrary to the faith. This precaution may have had reference to the tonsure or the Easter question or to matters connected with the liturgy; but it seems more probable that it was feared that this theologian from the East might not hold the orthodox side in the monothelite controversy which was then vexing the Church.

Theodore arrived in England in the year 669, being then sixty-seven years old. The paschal controversy had been settled by the conference at Whitby; the paganism of the Anglo-Saxons was practically gone; but the English Church was in a depressed condition. The succession introduced by Augustine survived only in the person of Boniface of East Anglia, who died within a year; and there were but three bishops engaged in active duties in England: Wilfrid, consecrated for York but officiating in Kent; Chad, occupying York in what was held to be an irregular way as to both consecration and jurisdiction; and Wina, who had been expelled from Wessex and had, by purchase, procured for himself the see of London. It was no small task which lay before this man of scholarly habits, who had spent all his life in monasteries in southern Europe. But Theodore, a very gift of God to England, was equal to the work. He made a visitation of the whole country; he consecrated bishops to vacant sees; he restored Wilfrid to York and Lindisfarne; he supplied (as we are told) the defects in Chad's consecration— it is impossible to say just what the words mean —and gave him a bishopstool at Lichfield; and he became in a sense the sole ecclesiastical ruler of England more than a century before it was all subjected to the rule of one king.

In the autumn of 673, some four years and a half after his arrival in England, Theodore summoned his suffragans to meet him at Hertford. Chad was dead; Wilfrid was represented by deputies; Wina did not attend; and the four bishops who sat with Theodore appear to have been all of his own consecration. The archbishop called upon them to accept the definitions of the faith, and discussed with them certain canons relating to the organization and the administration of the Church under a diocesan system, and to other like matters; then the decrees were formulated, signed, and promulgated. It is impossible to overestimate the importance of the council thus solemnly assembled, and of the work which it did. It gave unity and form to the English Church by providing it with a synodical system, from the lack of which its organization had thus far been imperfect, even as compared with that of the British Church in Wales; it made England an ecclesiastical province, having a unity of life and work and common interests; and, more than that, it gave to Englishmen the idea of a unity which afterwards found embodiment under kings of all England. It was, as the historians confess, "the first of all national gatherings for general legislation," and "the precursor of the Witenagemots and parliaments of the one indivisible imperial realm." The acts which made the bishops heads of dioceses rather than general missionaries, and governors in a national Church rather than chaplains of petty princes, had no little influence in the making of England. From Theodore and his council at Hertford went forth the inspiration which consolidated the realm, which gave the bishops seats in the meetings of the kings' wise men, which led to the assembling of the Commons at Westminster, and which has secured to England a unique place among the Churches and the kingdoms of the world.

Thus Theodore had done much to perfect the organization and external form of the English Church. He was strongly convinced himself that it was absolutely necessary for its welfare that the number of dioceses should be largely increased, though as to this point he had not been able to persuade his first council to take definite action. But he watched his opportunities; and he did his best to carry out plans like those of Gregory for the division of the land into comparatively small dioceses. It was in consequence of resistance to these plans that Wilfrid, as we have seen, fell into disfavor with the archbishop, and carried his appeal to Rome; and probably for a like reason the successor of Chad in the large diocese of Lichfield was removed from his see. In 685, Theodore, then eighty-three years old, was in York and was assisted by seven bishops in consecrating Cuthbert to Lindisfarne; and before this time he seems to have accomplished his wish in regard to the increase of the number of dioceses. Five years later, at the great age of eighty-eight, he died, and was buried in Augustine's monastery in his cathedral city.

As we have seen, he had organized and given unity to the English Church, and had prepared the way for the unity of the English nation; and in doing this he had secured for the Church of England a dignified and honored place among the Churches of Christendom. He had divided all the southern and eastern part of the island into permanent dioceses, largely on the lines of the ancient kingdoms; and he had prepared the way for the introduction of the parochial system, which tradition indeed ascribes to him, but which, in its details, is certainly the work of a later generation. Nor must we forget the impulse which he gave to learning. Himself no mean scholar, he founded schools of learning at Canterbury and elsewhere, where Greek and mathematics, as well as theology and canon law, were studied; he left behind him a penitential, which bears witness to the way in which he contended with the practical evils of his time; and to the impulse given by his devotion and his diligence is doubtless due much of the missionary zeal which marks the time that followed him. "Both his character and his work," writes the Bishop of Oxford, "seem to place him among the first and the greatest of the saints whom God has used for the building up of the Church and the development of the culture of the world."

On lines thus marked out the English Church went on with its work. We have noted how its development preceded that of the kingdom, and how it gave a tone to the national life rather than received one from it. It may not be amiss to remind ourselves how much this means. For although, as has been said, the early bishops may seem to have been little more than court-chaplains, yet the Christianity of our Anglo-Saxon ancestors was not a court-religion; nor, on the other hand, was the Church obliged to take up the position of a defender of the people against the tyranny of their rulers. There was a strong democratic element in those little kingdoms, which indeed the Teutonic emigrants had brought with them from their former homes; and politically the town preceded the kingdom; the realm of England, like the states of New England and the nation of the United States, was a growth from beneath. But the Church of England was a growth from above; the diocese preceded the parish; the bishop had a general jurisdiction, and his clergy were rather missionaries at large until duties were assigned them by the bishop, acting on the nomination of the lords of manors, over their respective parishes, the limits of which depended upon those of the towns. And many of the bishopstools were not in great and important places, and the civil capital has never been the metropolitical city. Moreover, the clergy of England have from the first been a part of the people, and have not formed a separate caste, with different civil interests. And so it has happened that the religious life and the religious organization of the country have remained through many political changes, and that the influence of bishops and clergy has been constantly good and constantly respected. Thus, while all the rest of Western Christendom accepted imperialism in Church and in State, England always claimed, and nearly always maintained, her independence; the freedom of the Church constantly defended the freedom of the State.

IV.

Upon the completion of the organization of the English Church there followed, as has been suggested, a time of quiet growth and of devotion to learning. The name which stands out prominently now is that of Bede, of whom all succeeding generations have spoken as the Venerable ; his home for fifty-four years was in the monastery at Jarrow, near the Scottish boundary. His was a life of quiet diligence, unambitious and affectionate, the only wish of which was to do something which would be of use. If he studied and wrote theology, it was that he might make the learning of the fathers of avail for the needs of his countrymen ; if he committed the history of his own day to writing, it was that he might bear witness to future generations of what God had done. With a charming simplicity, an unaffected patriotism, and an unfailing faith, he used his abilities for the glory of his Master and for the good of the Church ; and his name well stands to-day, where he could never have expected to see it, at the very beginning of the long line of English writers. Few scenes are more touching than that of his death on the eve of the Ascension-day ; as in the neighboring chapel they were about to sing the antiphon, " We beseech Thee leave us not orphans," he roused himself to dictate the last words of his English version of St. John's Gospel, and then, as the music of the choir reached his ears, he began the *Gloria*, and " breathed his last when he had named the Holy Spirit." Nor may we forget Caedmon, the rustic Northumbrian, who believed that he was divinely taught to sing, and who told in the simple rhythm of that day the story of the Scriptures and of God's dealings with men; nor how the close of the life of this first of English poets, told by the first of English historians, so closely resembles that which another should soon tell of Bede himself. And, though he did not write in the vernacular, England must ever honor Alcuin, the great theologian of the cathedral school at York, called by Charles the Great to his court, the restorer of learning in France and Germany, a man remarkable alike as a teacher and as a writer. These men, and those who were associated with them, were the crown of English learning in the eighth century.

As a restorer of learning some two centuries later, it may not be unfitting to speak here of King Alfred, successor of the Egbert of Wessex who founded the one kingdom of England. He was, says a great historian, "the most perfect character in history—a saint without superstition, a scholar without ostentation, a warrior all of whose wars were fought in defence of his country, a conqueror whose laurels were never stained by cruelty, a prince never cast down by adversity, never lifted up by insolence in the hour of triumph." "His virtue," proceeds the same writer, "like the virtues of Washington, consisted in no marvellous displays of superhuman genius, but in the simple, straightforward discharge of the duty of the moment." In all his life and his work he was a veritable nursing-father of the Church of England. But the Church owes him most for his devotion to learning and his determination that all his people should well understand what was written in their own tongue. He himself translated and enriched Boethius and Orosius and Bede, and gave a new tone to the Anglo-Saxon Chronicle. With him, in one sense, English history, as the history of one people, begins; with him, too, in an important sense, English literature has its beginning; and Alfred was the father of the English people, and has a name high among English writers, because he was a faithful son of the English Church.

But before Alfred's day the Danish invasions had begun, and the quiet life of England, especially in the north, had been disturbed. In those troubled times, great names do not rise up before us as in the days of foundation and growth at which we have been glancing. The time was drawing near when a conqueror was to come from without, and while he should not put an end to either the political or the ecclesiastical life of England, should yet produce a change so important that it might well be called a revolution. Of the preparations for the changes, which really have not much to do with the history of the early English Church, it is not necessary to speak here and now.

But one would be doing scant justice to that Church who should not have a word to say in regard to what was done by the missionaries whom, in the days of her early faith, she sent out to the heathen. We need not wonder that men went from Kent to Essex and to Sussex, or from Northumbria to Mercia, to tell their neighbors of the truth which had been brought to them; and perhaps the labors of Wilfrid, when he preached to the Frisians and to the men of Wessex, may seem to us no more than the work of an energetic but disappointed man, who felt that he must be laboring somewhere; in reality, however, these were but examples of what the Church of the Angles and the Saxons in England seems to have been always ready to do. Willibrord, educated at Ripon by Wilfrid and later in Ireland, filled with a missionary inspiration, became the apostle of the Frisians, and preached to the Danes and the Franks, and became the Archbishop of Utrecht. And Winfrid of Wessex, known to history as Boniface, longing for the labors of a missionary's life, became the apostle of Germany, worked most indefatigably and successfully, attained great honor and influence, gained a martyr's crown, and left an example to those who came after him.

V.

It is well that the story of the early English Church, which began with events so strangely combining the romantic with the miraculous, should end with a person about whom there gather stories of romance and of miracle. It was a wonderful change that took place from the time when a Frankish princess, with her chaplain, worshipped in the little St. Martin's Church at Canterbury, to the time when the fair minster of West London rose in place of the humbler edifice built by the first Christian king of Essex on Thorney Island near the Thames; a wonderful change from Ethelbert the heathen lord of Kent to Edward the sainted king of England. The light which blazed up at one place and another among Angles and Saxons and Jutes had illumined the whole land, and, though dimmed by the violence of enemies, had never ceased to burn. And now that a great change was to take place, the devotion of the last king of Saxon England (if one may use the phrase) showed itself in his determination to complete what he considered the great duty of his life. For fourteen years he pushed the work on the great abbey at Westminster, some of the foundations and arches of which are still seen beneath or near the more glorious building with which a later age has replaced it. The Witan of all England met to hallow the new minster on the Innocents' Day of the year 1065; but the king, who had appeared in public on the preceding day, was not able to be present. Before the Christmas festivities were over, he was stricken with death; and on the festival of the Epiphany, 1066, "the last royal son of Woden was borne to his grave." It may be that Edward was not a great man or a great ruler; it may be that it would have been better for his kingdom and no worse for himself if he had devoted his energies to something besides the erection of a stately church in the hope that he might thereby secure the salvation of his soul; but whose heart is not touched as he thinks of the king of England, who, on the very eve of the Norman conquest, was laid to rest in the shrine which he had just completed? Who that sees the receptacle of his ashes, alone of all the feretories of English saints, still in a place of honor in the house of God, and that remembers the reverence with which generations have treated it, does not feel that, after all, there was something appropriate in the time of the death of Edward the Confessor and in the place of his burial? And when we think that the great abbey is the resting-place of a long line of kings, successors of Ethelbert and Alfred and Edward, though not because they were of their blood, and that there lie under the same roof the bones of the good and the great and the wise who have entered into the labors of the good and great and wise of the earlier days— when we recall the constant worship which has been offered in that hallowed spot, and how holy men have stood in their place to guide the devotions and instruct the souls of a Christian English people through all these centuries—when we see the glorious chapter-house, so long the place of meeting of England's Commons, and the palace of Westminster hard by which now supplies its place, where are carried out the principles of government which found expression in the council at Hertford and in the assemblies in which the kings consulted with their bishops and their lords—who does not feel that the history of the earlier England fitly passes at Westminster with hardly a break into the history of the later England, from St. Edward the English Confessor to William the Norman Conqueror?

I have thus ventured to trace out the history of the Anglo-Saxon Church by reminding you of Augustine at Canterbury, of Wilfrid at Whitby, of Theodore at Hertford, of Bede at Jarrow, and of King Edward at Westminster. The scenes at which we have looked may have served to remind us how archbishops and kings, missionaries and scholars, monks and statesmen, worked together in the making of the Church of England. And the whole of the period which belongs to our subject this evening is full of like events, less prominent perhaps, but no less really affecting the centuries that were to follow. At times the story may suggest to us that good men often do things which call for an apology, and that it may not be well to criticise too closely the characters and the actions of some of those whom we honor with the title of saints; but on the other hand we cannot refrain from paying the tribute of reverential respect to those simple-hearted and faithful kings and bishops, for whom religion was the whole of life, and who gladly served the Lord Christ from love of Him Who had saved them. And it was—who can doubt it?—because of the completeness of their devotion that their " work of faith and labour of love and patience of hope " were so evidently accepted and blessed. As we read Homer with an ever-increasing sense of the beauty of " the dawn of history's morning," as there always breathes from the verses of Chaucer the sweet freshness of the spring of poetry, so as we follow the chronicles of the days when Christianity was brought into the England and to the Englishmen of history, we get much of the inspiration of that loving devotion and patient faith which we hardly dare hope to find reproduced in our own times. We see our holy religion accepted by warlike Teutonic tribes, without the intervention of force or arms, simply because it was quiet and self-denying and pure; we see it changing their temper towards the Britons whom they had driven from their homes, because they had, though from another source, received the faith of their conquered foes; we see it making the numerous kingdoms of Angles and Saxons and Jutes into one nation, the national unity being based upon the ecclesiastical; we see the Britons drawn with the English into the visible unity of the Catholic Church of the West; and we see the Church of England maintaining her rights as a branch of the Church Catholic against the already immoderate claims of the see of Rome. And we see the light of learning which had flashed from the emerald plains of Ireland and from the rocks of Iona, shining now from England and dispelling the darkness which had begun to settle on portions of the continent. And thus we see the English Church, strong in faith and wise in holy learning, able to bear the shocks which were to come upon it and to defend the sacred deposit of faith and order which it had received. It is indeed no ordinary history which we have been studying, as we have watched the building of a plain but solid substructure, which rests firmly upon the one foundation than which man can lay no other, and which supports in safety a stately pile that ministers to the needs of human souls and echoes with the unceasing praises of Almighty God.

The Norman Period of the English Church.

LECTURE III.

BY ALEXANDER V. G. ALLEN, D.D.,
Professor in the Episcopal Theological School, in Cambridge, Mass.

THE NORMAN PERIOD OF THE ENGLISH CHURCH.

THE Norman people came to England with William the Conqueror in 1066. Their first appearance in Europe dates from the middle of the ninth century, or some two hundred years earlier than their conquest of England. They came from the Scandinavian countries in the north, what are now the kingdoms of Denmark, Sweden and Norway. They were a fierce and warlike people, whose empire was the sea. At a time when, to the other people of Europe, the ocean was a barrier of separation, it was to the Normans a highway and channel of communication. Leaving their homes in the north, in the ninth century they had gone into France and taken possession of that province now known as Normandy. In the early part of the eleventh century they had wandered into the south, where they had made themselves masters of southern Italy, including Sicily. In their love of conquest they had also discovered and settled Iceland, they had planted colonies in Greenland, and by some it is believed that they had landed in North America, and had even made some settlement on the coast of New England.*

The Normans were a Teutonic people, and therefore closely related by blood to the English and the Germans. But close as may be the race connection, the difference between them and the other Teutonic races is great and striking. Their peculiarities are brought out most clearly in France, where they had been settled for two hundred years before the conquest of England. They had taken on the refinements of civilization, as civilization then was; they threw themselves

---

* It is a mistake, however, to speak of the Northmen as having *discovered* America. The word *discovery* in its true historical use applies only to Europe in the sixteenth century —to the age and people which were waiting to carry on the advancing civilization. A discovery also implies some conscious, intelligent purpose, not an accidental stumbling upon a territory, which incident was, moreover, followed by no result. If it were right to speak of the Northmen as having *discovered* America, it would be still more correct to speak of the Indians as its first discoverers; and then it might as well be admitted that it was never discovered at all. It was always known to some people or race as far back as history reaches.

into the life of the continent, and whatever was in vogue at the time they appropriated as their own, and carried out to its full development. Just as they had conquered for themselves a home in countries which did not belong to them, so they also entered into the life of the age, accepting its features, its ideals, its lines of movement with as genuine an enthusiasm as if they had originated them from their own consciousness. They became the most devoted adherents of the papacy to be found in Europe. In Italy, so great was their reverence for the Bishop of Rome, they formed a sort of body-guard to the pope, taking an oath to defend the papacy against all its foes. Hildebrand found them most useful allies in the maintenance of his policy for subjecting the States of Europe to the obedience of the Church. The Normans being, as it were, a people without a home, were emancipated from local or national restrictions; they were cosmopolitans, cherishing what was large and universal in scope or tendency, with an admiration for power and splendor without reference to its national bearings. They were an imaginative people, instinctively giving themselves up to the cultivation of art, which then assumed the phase of architecture. The cathedrals, the monasteries, the churches which rose in Normandy may be regarded as expressing their religious and imaginative genius. More than any other part of Europe did Normandy abound in ecclesiastical foundations after the model of the rising Gothic style, which there reached its fullest growth, producing monuments of beauty which are unexcelled.

When the crusades began in the end of the eleventh century, whose object was the chivalrous attempt to recover the Holy Sepulchre at Jerusalem from the hand of the infidel Moslem, it was the Normans who were foremost in responding to the call of the pope, and who first planted themselves as conquerors in the sacred city. And, indeed, throughout the crusades, it is either the Normans or peoples of the Latin races, *not Germans or English*, who are chiefly identified with this vast movement in the interest of an ideal purpose. Let us add that the Normans were a peculiarly religious people in what are called *the ages of faith*. Here, too, they showed the same disposition as in other things. They accepted the forms of the monastic life as expressing the highest type of sanctity and devotion. Wherever they went, they built magnificent monasteries as they built magnificent churches, every great feudal lord, it is said, planting a monastic establishment upon his domain. The Normans easily subscribed the monastic vows of chastity, poverty and obedience, sacrificing that element of being or existence which we call vitality or vigorous personality, as readily as they also sacrificed home and nationality in the love of what was foreign, or splendid, or cosmopolitan.

Here lay also their weakness. Nowhere did they build up a nation. It has been their fate to be merged in other peoples; they have disappeared in Italy; in France and in England they have been fused with the original population. The test of a people's vitality is seen in the retention of their language; Germany and England have shown the purity and tenacity of their original stock by retaining their language, despite all foreign influences. The Normans gave up their own language for the language of the people they conquered. Not only did they fail to build up a nation; they weakened by their emigration the countries which were their original homes, so that Denmark and Sweden and Norway lost the future which might have been theirs, and have never played an important part in the history of Europe.

Such were the people who came over into England from Normandy in France, with William the Conqueror in the year 1066. A greater contrast than that between the English—the Anglo-Saxons, as they are generally called—and the Norman conquerors it is hard to imagine. Hitherto England had taken little part in the great movements going on upon the Continent. The insulated character of the country showed itself in the insulation and exclusiveness which marks the character of the people. England pursued its own way through the early Middle Ages, unaffected by the changes in France, or Germany, or Italy. She knew but little of the ambition of popes, or the methods by which the Bishop of Rome was recasting into legislation the moral sentiment which went forth toward his person as the Vicar of Christ upon earth. Church and State in England during the Anglo-Saxon period, were in harmonious relations. No one was then asking the momentous question of a later age, whether the Church should rule the State, or the State the Church; it was hard to tell them apart, as when the dignitaries of Church and State met in one common assembly, legislating alike for the *Ecclesia* or the nation. There was a form of monasticism in England, but it was of the mildest type, not adhering to the Benedictine rule. The clergy also were for the most part married, nor did their conception of the Christian ideal lead to the exaggeration of celibacy, as the equivalent of chastity. There was, in a word, nothing cosmopolitan about the English; they were then, as they have been ever since, a practical people, cherishing no visionary schemes, not endowed with a glowing imagination, rude in their architecture, their prevailing sin, it is often remarked, being gluttony—a type of pleasure which they indulged in at their numerous and hospitable feasts.

All this was changed by the coming of the Normans. The conquest was so complete that England now wheels into line as one of the papal states of Europe, accepting more entirely than almost any other country the authority of the Bishop of Rome, taking on foreign fashions, and embroiled in the politics of Christendom. The change was easily effected. William, the Norman conqueror, had received the approval and even the blessing of the pope on his attempt to subjugate the English people, and to take possession of their crown, sailing for England, it is said, with a banner blessed for the undertaking by Alexander, the Bishop of Rome. It is unnecessary to recount here the details of the story of his conquest. The resistance which he met with from the English people was overcome by a fierce and cruel determination to make the country entirely his own. He assumed from the first the feudal principle that all the land belonged to him by sovereign right; he proceeded at once to dispossess its English owners and to assign their estates to his Norman followers. Although the process was a gradual one, it went on, until the ejection of a great nation of landowners from their land was accomplished. Nor was all this effected without enormous suffering. "No book in the world," it has been said, "covers so huge a mass of misery, thinly disguised under its cold, curt phraseology, as the great terrier of the Norman king's English estate," to which the English people gave the name of Domesday. A Norman nobility now displaced the Englishmen of high rank, who sank into the lower grades of tenants; the Episcopal seats throughout England were filled with Norman bishops, with only one exception; the English Archbishop of Canterbury was removed, and in his room was placed an Italian, Lanfranc, who came from the monastery of Bec, in Normandy. There were two races in the land, the English and the French, as the Normans called themselves. The Normans despised the Anglo-Saxons, looking down with contempt upon their rude and narrow ways, while the English or Saxons returned their contempt with bitter hatred In consequence of the frequent assassinations of the Normans, a law was framed which made the local hundred responsible for every murder if the murderer was not found, while every murdered man was held to be a Norman, unless he could be proved to be an Englishman.

This was the age when the great castles were erected all over England. The traveller who admires to-day their beauty as a feature of the English landscape does not trouble himself to recall their origin. The hard and cruel necessities of a former age become the luxuries and playthings of later generations. These castles were built by the Normans in self-defence; they dominated the country around; they were the strongholds of Norman tyranny and rapine. Horrors were perpetrated in their dungeons which never saw the light of day.

"Every powerful man," says the last English chronicler, "built his castle, and they filled the land full of castles. They heavily afflicted the poor men of the land with castle-building, and when the castles were built they filled them with devils and evil men. Then, both by night and day, they took the men they supposed to possess any goods, country men and women, and threw them into prison, to obtain their gold and silver and torture them with unutterable torture, for never were martyrs tortured as they were. . . . They were constantly levying tributes on the towns; and when the wretched men had no more to give, they destroyed and burnt the towns; and well might you travel all day and never find a man settled in a town or land cultivated, so that corn was dear; of flesh and cheese and butter none was there in the land. Wretched men starved of hunger. Some went begging through the country who formerly had been rich men. Some fled the country. Never was greater wretchedness in the land and never did heathen men cause worse evils than these did. So that men said openly that Christ and His saints were asleep."

The old England came to an end under the Norman kings, and these are the last words of the Anglo-Saxon chronicler.

The Norman lords built their castles and the Norman bishops raised their great cathedrals. These wonderful structures, like the castles, have now become almost a constituent part of English scenery. The English nation has forgotten the misery of their origin. Even nature itself has accepted them, as if man, in rivalry with the work of the Creator, had done something of which the heavens, that look down upon them, might be proud. The cathedrals of the Norman bishops, even the churches in towns and villages, the splendid monasteries, are relics of the Norman conquest. The older churches of the Anglo-Saxon period were destroyed to make place for the grander architecture; only a few remain to tell us what they were like; they were despised by the Normans because they were small. But even with all their beauty and splendor and vast proportions, these things are not the typical utterance of the English mind. Even if we forget their origin, Durham, and Canterbury, and Salisbury, and Winchester still remind us of the age when England became for the first time in her history a constituent part of Roman Catholic Christendom, gradually learning to forget the simplicity of her earlier Church, in the grandeur and comprehensiveness of the papal empire.

Other features of the period might be interesting and instructive to study, especially the fill-ing up of England with the various branches of monasticism, which the foreign invaders brought with them from France or Italy. For it is a circumstance not without its significance, that no great monastic order has ever originated in England. The Cistercian order, the order of Clugny, the order of the Carthusians or of the Carmelites, at a later time the mendicant orders, Franciscan and Dominican, none of these sprang from the religious genius or aspiration of the English Church; they were importations from Italy or France or Spain. Their monastic houses were endowed with all the imaginative beauty of the Norman mind; their sites reveal a wonderful appreciation of the beauty of nature, and the English people are still proud of their ruins. Furness and Fountains and Melrose and hundreds of others, we may admit, did good in their day; for the Normans as monks were a better people than the lay lords who built the castles. But these institutions are not indigenous to English soil; they do not reflect the characteristic religious life or purpose of the English people. The time came when the English nation swept them away, while hardly a voice was heard to protest in their behalf.

Of all these foreign institutions and methods, one general remark holds true—they enlarged the spirit of the English Church. There were in them seeds of evil, but there were also seeds of good.

Feudalism, for example, which was introduced into England with the Normans, though in a modified shape, cultivated a spirit of loyalty to an over-lord which, when transferred to Christ, becomes the source of what is most beautiful and vital in Christian piety. The customs of chivalry, also brought in by the Normans, elevated the tone of manners, raised the ideal of woman, cultivated the sense of personal honor, which forms not only an integral element in the character of what we call the gentleman, but an indispensable element in all moral culture. Influences like these lifted the Church of England out of its natural exclusiveness. Left to itself the English Church might have become a stunted, narrow institution, feebly reflecting the spirit of Christianity, feebly nourishing the life of the nation,—not unlike the Russian Church of to-day, which in all its history has received no life from without, and sits weak and powerless at the feet of the Czar.

Of these institutions and ideals which are foreign to the typical English mind, the most important is the papacy. It was the leading consequence of the Norman invasion that England was made an organic part of the Latin or Roman Catholic Church, accepting the headship of the pope over the State as well as over the Church. How the process of its conquest by the pope was accomplished, what were the effects on the English

Church and nation, how at last this yoke was thrown off, is the story I propose to tell.

Before the Norman conquest, and during the Anglo-Saxon age, there existed in England, as on the continent, a feeling of respect and deference for the Bishop of Rome. He was regarded as the successor of St. Peter, and St. Peter was believed to have been the head or prince of the apostles. So early as the eighth century English bishops had begun to take an oath of allegiance to the Bishop of Rome. Indeed, the first bishop who ever took such an oath was an Englishman, St. Boniface, known as the missionary apostle of Germany. When he left England for Germany to convert the new races from heathenism, he felt the need of some centre, some responsible head to whom he might offer his Christian conquests, and thus connect them with a larger Church than the local body which he represented. This act of Boniface may be regarded as one illustration out of many, of the working of that moral sentiment of reverence for the Bishop of Rome which existed among all the people of western Europe.

But the Latin Church has never been content with moral sentiments. They seem to the Latin mind vague, intangible things, until they have been transmuted into the form of law. During the eighth and ninth centuries, or in the age when Charlemagne was sole ruler of the new western empire, the process went on apace, of converting this sentiment of reverence for Rome into legal statutes, by means of which the bishops of Rome might govern the Church in accordance with what they believed to be the will of God. Rome was in the habit of gratifying the sentiment of reverence toward her ancient see, by presenting to the bishops, on their consecration, the pallium, as a token of her recognition of their office, —a badge of their relationship through Rome to the universal Church. In that confused and struggling age, when the nations had not yet been born, and in the isolation of the peoples no other bond of unity existed, the presentation of the pallium was a glimpse into a larger world, revealing a grander Church behind the local Churches in the various kingdoms or states of western Europe.

When the bishops who received the pallium took the oath of allegiance to Rome, a great step forward had been accomplished in the process of subjecting the Church to the will of Rome. But still, the oath was a vague one, and meant little or much as any bishop might choose to interpret it. In order to give the bishop's oath any real import, it was necessary to define by legal statute how much it meant. The popes who inherited the spirit of the old Roman law, were at no loss to determine the form which the legislation should take. It was necessary, as they thought, for the government of the Church, that the papacy should constitute a court of final appeal in all grave cases in which the bishops might be concerned. The bishops were encouraged to appeal to Rome under the conviction that their causes would be more justly adjudged, than if they were decided by some archbishop, or metropolitan, or were referred to the king's court.

But how to accomplish this result was the difficulty. In those days, men did not reason upon the subject and enact a law because it was in accordance with justice or right. It was necessary to show, if possible, that such had always been the law of the Church from the time of the apostles. If the origin of law could be buried in the mists of antiquity, beyond which no eye could reach, then the reverence for it could be based upon a divine right which none would dispute.

There were those in the ninth century who were equal to the emergency. It is sad to relate that the papacy—the only high and universal ideal of the middle ages—was driven to build up its legal power over the Church by the most stupendous fraud which is known to history. There appeared suddenly in Germany, about the middle of the ninth century, a code of laws for the government of the Church, in which it was made to appear that the popes had possessed the right of hearing appeals from the very time of the apostles. The first bishops of Rome, after St. Peter, were there represented as claiming this power in explicit decretals; and as they stood on the threshold of the apostolic age, and embodied its spirit, the inference followed that the appellate jurisdiction of Rome rested upon divine right, eternal and irrefragable as the law of Christ. The forgery was complete and successful. No one denied or disputed its authenticity; no one was learned enough to expose the falsehoods or anachronisms with which the " forged decretals " abounded ; the popes accepted them as a law for the justification of their action.

It might be an interesting question to discuss what would have been the fortunes of the papacy without the forged decretals. It is doubtful if its history could have been the same. In this age it is hard to make allowance for institutions which call themselves divine and which yet make use of deception to accomplish their ends. We need not ask in this case where the responsibility of the falsehood lies. Of course, primarily upon the monk who, in the silence and secrecy of his cell, forged the document which received universal credence upon its appearance. Of the inner history of the forgery we know but little, nor is it certain that the popes knew it to be a fraud. This pretended legislation fell in so naturally and easily with what they believed ought to have been the law of the Church, that they may be pardoned for the willing credulity with which they accepted and acted upon its principles. And Europe for the most part was also in the same situation.

Two hundred years had passed away since the forged decretals appeared and the bishops of Rome had made little or no progress toward the accomplishment of their ideal vision. They desired to see the Church in Europe one vast organization, governed by a responsible head, who should be strong enough to protect the clergy everwhere in the exercise of their sacred functions, strong enough to resist encroachments upon their rights, courageous to speak for truth and righteousness despite the opposition of all earthly powers. In the eleventh century, the age of the Norman conquest, there rose up a pope, in some respects the master mind of his age—a man who would have been famous in any age. Hildebrand, or by his ecclesiastical title Pope Gregory VII., controlled the policy of Rome for thirty years before he assumed the tiara. It is supposed that William the Conqueror had papal permission to make the conquest of England through Hildebrand's influence, and that the reigning pope was merely his spokesman. Hildebrand deserves to be called great, because he read his age so clearly. He saw that the Church could never become an universal Christian empire, a theocracy accomplishing the will of God on earth, unless the civil power, the princes, the kings and emperors were first made subject to its control. Everywhere he looked he saw that the State stood in the way of the Church. Because the Church had grown rich in lands and revenues, it was a constant temptation to kings and princes to use the Church and its endowments in order to secure civil ends. It seemed to Hildebrand as if the Church were desecrated and robbed of its divine strength, by having any connection with the State. As he reasoned on the subject, the spiritual was higher and more important than the secular or worldly, the ecclesiastical interests were eternal while those of the State were temporal. The policy outlined in his far-seeing mind was a stupendous effort for one man to attempt. He saw that the Church must first be separated from the State, owning no connection with or allegiance to the civil power; and then that the States of Europe must be made subject to the direct power of God on earth, as represented by the Bishop of Rome. It was another mark of the greatness of Hildebrand that he believed in the success of an effort to accomplish this vast revolution. Hildebrand combined the capacity of the most astute of politicians, with the mood of a divine dreamer, who lives not for himself, but for God. In his words, contained in the bull by which he excommunicated the German emperor, we have revealed to us the extent of his ambitious purpose: "Come, now, I pray you, O most Holy Father, and princes (Peter and Paul), that all the world may know that if you are able to bind and loose in heaven, you are able on earth to take away or to give to each according to his merits, empires, kingdoms, duchies, marquisates, counties and the possessions of all men." Hildebrand was sincere in his belief that this power had been committed to him, and that to resist his will was to defy the authority of God. He stands at the beginning of a new era in Europe, the age of the papal supremacy, a dominion which endured for 300 years. With this age coincides the Norman period in the history of the Church of England. It shall be in England that we follow the popes, until they achieve their purpose.

The first step which was taken toward separating the Church from the State was the enforcement of clerical celibacy—an ideal of the Middle Ages which had not yet been realized. So long as the clergy were married they would be interested in the fortunes of the State and dependent upon the well-being of the State for the advancement of themselves and their children; but a celibate clergy, having no interest in the State, would become devoted exclusively to the Church. Up to this time the clergy in England had for the most part been married. Hildebrand's decree of celibacy was carried out against their will; and though there must have been more exceptions to its enforcement in England than elsewhere, it became the law of the English Church. The Norman conqueror in this respect sympathized with the papal policy, as did also his Norman followers. They brought with them to England the idea prevailing upon the Continent, that duty to the Church demanded this sacrifice of all who ministered at its altars.

There was also another law which Hildebrand promulgated, and which he was not so successful in enforcing, at least in England—a law the promulgation of which gave rise to a long and violent controversy, known as the Investiture Controversy. We shall better understand its nature by following the course of events in England.

Although William the Conqueror had procured the approval of the pope for the conquest of England, yet after he was established there he did not propose that the pope should interfere with his authority. The pope also was prudent, and refrained from interfering with William, while he violated the law, for whose infraction he dared to excommunicate the Emperor of Germany. The theory on which William governed England is known as Feudalism. It assumed that all the lands of the country belonged to the king. The king had given these lands to his subjects on certain conditions, among the foremost of which was the understanding that the tenant or vassal should aid the king in his wars, by furnishing a certain contingent of soldiers equipped for his army. The great question of the hour was whether the Church lands should also be held on the same tenure. Were the bishops and the heads of great monasteries, the king's men, and were they also bound in return for lands which they held, to render the vassal's service and to aid the monarch with their revenues? If the spiritual nobility, like the secular lords, were vassals to the king, then it followed that lands and other property which had been given to the Church still belonged primarily to the king. It was the king's pleasure to allot these lands to the Church on fixed conditions, and these conditions implied that the archbishop or bishop should do homage to the king in order to be invested with the dignities and revenues of their sees. It must be remembered that at this time in England the Church held nearly one-third of all the lands of the kingdom. The king would have felt impoverished and unable to carry on his constant wars, or to reward his subjects who had done him service, had one-third of his territory been alienated from his control.

William the Conqueror had no doubt upon the question. He claimed the Church's lands as belonging to the crown. He regarded the bishops as great feudatories quite as truly as the secular lords. He proceeded to put his friends and servants in possession of the lands of the Church without much regard to their spiritual fitness for the position. The bishops became courtiers, holding by feudal tenure, and the only distinction between them and the secular lords was the attaching of what were called spiritual duties to the conditions on which they were entitled to their office and revenues. But the qualification for spiritual duties came last. In the impressive ceremonial by which, as Mr. Freeman has shown, the bishops qualified for their position, first came the act of homage to the king, in which the bishop designate, kneeling before the king and placing his hands in the king's hands, swore to be an obedient vassal to his overlord. The act of homage was followed by the enthronement or investiture, when the king presented him with the staff and ring as the symbols of his office. After these ceremonies he was spiritually qualified in the act of consecration by bishops who represented the Church's part in the transaction. It shows how great the change is which has since taken place, that in the present method of making a bishop in the English Church, consecration by the bishops comes first, then follows the enthronement or investiture with the dignities and revenues of the see, and lastly comes the act of homage to the throne.

It was Hildebrand or Pope Gregory VII. who attempted to overcome this doctrine that the high dignitaries of the Church were the king's men. He regarded the property of the Church as belonging solely to God, and to the pope as the head of His Church in the world. The bishops were primarily the pope's men and not the king's men; they must be invested with the rights of their office by religious authority and not by the civil power. For the king to claim the Church's lands was robbery and sacrilege. For the bishop to allow himself to be invested with ring and staff by the secular power was to be guilty of simony, as when Simon Magus, in the apostles' time, sought to purchase the gifts of God with money.

Thus arose the great controversy about investiture, which lasted for more than a generation, and which finally ended in a compromise; for there was right on both sides of the question, and the papacy was unable to carry out Hildebrand's decree without some qualification of its sweeping purpose. Hildebrand had excommunicated and humiliated at Canossa the Emperor of Germany for daring to invest his bishops with the symbols of their office. But William the Conqueror was at a distance, strongly entrenched in his possession, and Hildebrand thought it imprudent to interfere. It would be unwise, even for him, to have more than one quarrel at a time with the monarchs of Europe. So William was left to his own devices. He filled up the sees of England at his pleasure, offering them as rewards to his faithful servants, who accepted them as a feudal tenure with their spiritual duties attached as a sort of secondary consideration.

William the Conqueror died in 1087. He was succeeded by his son, William II., or *William Rufus*, as he is generally called, who not only followed his father's policy in the matter of investiture, but went beyond his father in his claims of authority over the Church. The first William had lived on terms of amity with his archbishop Lanfranc, and both had labored together in the interest of consolidating the English nation. William the Conqueror, like David among the kings of Israel, had known how to adjust himself with the prophetic office as represented in the great see at Canterbury. Lanfranc, although an Italian, was a true yoke-fellow to his king, laboring with him for the strengthening of the kingly authority, and not neglectful of the well-being of the Church. We can hardly speak of England yet as a nation, but William and Lanfranc were unconsciously impelled by that subtle leaven of influence which had been an active force in earlier history, and which was destined to work until England should become foremost among the nations of the earth. We are chiefly impressed, as we study this period of English history, with the power and triumphs of the papacy, as it moved steadily on to the fulfilment of its purpose. And yet the real interest lies, not in this temporary sway of a theocratic emperor of Christendom, but in the silent and imperceptible steps by which the conquered English were assimilated to their Norman conquerors, until they became one people; the most absorbing study is to watch the process by which the English spirit vindicates itself against all foreign influences. And at last the English nation has come to the birth, richer and fuller for the invasions and humiliations which it has undergone.

But we must pause yet for a few moments longer upon this great duel between the English throne and the Roman pope before the utterance of the national consciousness is heard.*

William Rufus was inferior to his father not only as a king but as a man. He has been called the worst, the most thoroughly wicked king who

* There are several lives of Anselm, in which the story of his struggle with the crown is related; among others those of Dean Church, Rule, Hasse and Remusat. The best account, to which I am chiefly indebted, is given in Freeman's *History of William Rufus*, Vol. I.

ever wore the English crown. It is sometimes questioned whether there were any skepticisms in these ages of faith. But William Rufus was not only skeptical about religion, he was also a blasphemer and a hater of God, determined, as he expressed it, to have his vengeance upon God for all the evil that he suffered at His hands. He was not only this, but he was a man of the foulest life, introducing nameless vices into England which had been before unknown, except in the east and in the degraded times of the Roman Empire. It was a strange coincidence that such a man should be associated with an Archbishop of Canterbury like Anselm, the greatest saint of his age, the one man of all others who penetrated most deeply in that time into the higher mysteries of the Christian faith.

Anselm, too, was a foreigner, a native of Italy who, wandering away from his native village in Piedmont, had turned up in Normandy at the Monastery of Bec. When Lanfranc, its former abbot, was promoted to the See of Canterbury, Anselm had succeeded him as the head of the monastery. He had been known and liked by William the Conqueror, who had the gift, it is said, of discerning and loving men who were good at heart. In this way William Rufus had come to be acquainted with Anselm. If there was one redeeming trait in the character of William Rufus it was his reverence for the memory of his father. This fondness of his father for Anselm had something to do with his becoming the Primate of all England.

Anselm is generally known in Church history as the greatest theologian of the time, as a master in dialectics, and the founder of what is called the Scholastic philosophy. He is not generally associated with England in our minds, when we think of him in his theological and philosophical capacity. Perhaps England has no right to claim him as her own in this respect. For great as has been the history of the English Church, it has not been her mission to produce theologians of the highest order. Each nation has its special calling in the vineyard of God. It has been the work of Germany to produce great theologians rather than to create an ecclesiastical organization. The call of England has lain in the direction of building up a great national Church,—the reflex of the spiritual life of its people. As England gave birth to no great monastic orders, so her greatest theologian was also an importation from abroad, deriving his motive and his culture from a foreign source. But his connection with the English Church is nevertheless a close one, and the story of his relation to the line of our history is interesting in the highest degree.

William Rufus not only accepted his father's doctrine, that the lands of the Church belonged primarily to the crown, but he made a further application of the principle which shocked the moral sense of the people. Claiming for his own the lands and revenues of the sees and monasteries, he declared that it rested with his mere pleasure when they should be filled after the death of their occupants, or whether they should be filled at all. In case they were filled, it should be by those who were willing by rich presents and easy terms to make it an object for him to do so. After the death of Archbishop Lanfranc he allowed the See of Canterbury to remain vacant for five years, asserting his purpose to be his own archbishop. During these years he rented the lands of Canterbury to his own creatures, on his own terms, and appropriated to his own use the revenues. It seems as if he would have maintained this attitude throughout his reign, had he not been taken with a grievous sickness, which threatened his life and brought him to repentance. Under these circumstances he appointed Anselm, who happened to be in England at the time, as Archbishop of Canterbury, in the year 1093.

When Anselm became primate of all England, he did not share in the views which Hildebrand was proclaiming, that the Church should be separated from the State, and the State be subordinated to ecclesiastical rule He stipulated with the king that he would take the office, which he did not seek and did not want, on condition that the king would restore to the Church the possessions which had belonged to it in the days of his predecessor, Lanfranc. To this condition the king in his softened mood consented. Other conditions also Anselm had proposed, to which it is not so clear that the king assented—that the king would take him for his spiritual adviser, and also that he would recognize Pope Urban, who was then struggling with a rival claimant for the papal throne. So Anselm was made archbishop in the usual way, doing homage to the king and swearing obedience, receiving the ring and staff as symbols of his investiture with the possessions of his see, and then, lastly, consecrated by the bishops in order to his qualification for his spiritual functions.

Anselm had foreseen the difficulties which he would encounter in the execution of his office under such a king as William Rufus. He made use of an illustration which clearly shows how the two offices of king and primate then stood related to each other in the popular mind. "If," he remarked, "the field of the Church of England is to be cultivated, two of the strongest oxen must draw the plough,—the king and the archbishop, the former by his worldly authority and rule, the latter by spiritual instruction and guidance." He compared himself to an old and feeble sheep yoked to an ox in all the wildness of youth, and there would be danger that the ox would drag the sheep through hedges of thorns and brambles, until the lambs of the flock had perished. The significance of the illustration lies in this,—that Anselm allowed to the king an equal share with himself in the cultivation of the field of the Church of England. All this was soon to be changed, and Anselm was to become the agent of the change. I dwell upon the story because in it may be seen the transition of the popular sentiment by which the pope became supreme in England.

The repentance of William Rufus was not of long duration. When he recovered from his illness he fell back again to his evil ways. He refused to listen to Anselm, who remonstrated with him in his capacity as spiritual adviser; he robbed the Church in order to find means to carry on his sinful pleasures; he refused to fill the monasteries with abbots who would promote discipline; he neglected to appoint bishops and claimed the revenues of the vacant sees. When Anselm urged him to recognize Urban as pope he declined, for he wanted no interference from that source with his policy. At last, when Anselm asked permission to go to Rome to get the pallium, the token of his recognition by the Bishop of Rome, William refused his consent. It shows the character of the king, that, perceiving how Anselm had right on his side in this request, he finally sent to Rome secretly, recognized Urban and had the pallium brought to England by a papal messenger. At first it was proposed that Anselm should receive it at the hands of the king. When he declined to do this the pallium was laid on the altar of the great church at Canterbury, from whence Anselm took it with his own hands.

There was now a state of open rupture between the archbishop and the king. The king showed his displeasure in ways that annoyed his yoke-fellow and hindered his performance of his spiritual duty. He sent out of the country the friends and sympathizers of Anselm. He steadily refused to allow any synod to be held for the reformation of manners and discipline. Under these circumstances it is not strange that the soul of Anselm went through an inward transition which was typical of an impending revolution. He became hopeless of the situation and looked away from the kingdom for relief. He now began to muse upon the pope and his relation to the universal Church. "Rome seen at a distance seemed pure and holy; its pontiff seemed the one embodiment of right and law, the one shadow of God left upon the earth in a world of force and falsehood and wrong." It was a circumstance of deep significance for the fortunes of the English Church when Anselm fell to thinking about the pope. From that time the spirit of the man began to change. On three occasions he asked permission of the king to go to Rome, and each time the king, refusing his consent, grew more incensed against him. Then Anselm announced his intention to go without consent even though, as the king threatened, the archbishopric should be taken from him. On these terms the archbishop parted from the king.

William Rufus died while Anselm was absent an exile from his see. When Anselm returned he came back an altered man. He had seen something of the power of the Church abroad; he had embraced the theory of Hildebrand; he had participated in two councils at which secular investiture had been condemned, and those who dared perform it threatened with excommunication. When King Henry I., who succeeded William Rufus, demanded of Anselm the customary oath of allegiance in order that he might receive anew the archbishopric at his hands, Anselm refused to promise obedience and was again in open rupture with the royal authority. The mild and saintly man who had submitted so patiently to the insults of William Rufus now stood ready to excommunicate his successor for encroaching upon his spiritual authority. Under the moral influence of Anselm the sentiment grew in the kingdom that the king should have no part in cultivating the field of the Church. Spiritual things were for spiritual men. The Church, since it controlled spiritual and eternal destinies, must be independent of the State in order to realize its mission. It shows how the Church had gained on the State, that Anselm was able to hold the king in check by fear of ecclesiastical penalties. Had the Pope Paschal, come to the aid of the archbishop, the humiliation of the king might have been accomplished. But Paschal's situation, like that of Hildebrand, had its difficulties. Even the popes, claiming the supreme government of the world, were hampered by the limitations of worldly policy. The Emperor of Germany, Henry IV., was still giving the pope so much trouble that he was obliged to compromise the case between Henry of England, and his archbishop. Anselm did not carry his point. According to the terms of the compromise the king retained the really important part of investiture—the oaths of fealty and homage, while resigning the idle symbol of the gift of ring and crozier. But in the light of those intangible sentiments which govern the opinion of mankind, the Church had gained and the State had lost. It was a victory in itself, as the tides were then running, that an archbishop of Canterbury had defied the king of England and still retained possession of his see.

The Church had vindicated its spiritual independence, overcoming the danger which threatened it, of becoming a mere appanage of the crown. The gain was a real one for the cause of true religion, even though it inevitably promoted the civil supremacy of the Bishop of Rome.

The conflict of Anselm with the kings of England represents one stage in the process by which the popes achieved supremacy over the States of Europe. The principle at issue in this conflict had been the separation of the Church from the State in order to the freedom and independence of the Church. But hardly had this result been secured when the scene changes and the papacy appears as claiming that authority over the State which the State had been condemned for seeking to exercise over the Church. In following the steps of the process by which the popes attained their end in England, we are led to consider the question of ecclesiastical courts, which created the necessity of an appeal to the papacy as having supreme appellate jurisdiction.

In the happier adjustment of the relations of Church and State during the Anglo-Saxon period, there had been but one mode of legal procedure for clerics and for laymen. All cases were brought before a mixed tribunal composed of the highest ecclesiastical and lay dignitaries of the kingdom, to whose decision the clergy yielded as final no less than the laity. It was not thought improper that a layman should take part in adjudging questions which concerned the spiritual interests of the kingdom.

When William the Conqueror came to England, he brought with him another practice, which prevailed on the continent. He set up ecclesiastical courts presided over by bishops, with exclusive jurisdiction in the case of ecclesiastical offenders who were thus emancipated from secular tribunals. These spiritual or ecclesiastical courts have a curious history. They seem to have originated with the advice of St. Paul to the Corinthians:—

"Dare any of you, having a matter against his neighbor, to go to law before the unrighteous and not before the saints? Know ye not that the saints shall judge the world, and if the world shall be judged by you, are ye unworthy to judge the smallest matters? Know ye not that we shall judge angels, how much more things that pertain to this life? If then ye have to judge things pertaining to this life, do ye set them to judge who are of no account in the church? Is it so that there cannot be found among you one just man who shall be able to decide between his brethren, but brother goes to law with brother, and that before unbelievers?"

It was these words which became the warrant for the establishment of spiritual or ecclesiastical courts, in contrast with the civil or the king's courts. One hardly need stop to comment on the inapplicability of the apostle's words. They were spoken when the great world was heathen, when the Church formed a small circle of believers hemmed in by hostile sentiment. But after the world had become Christian, to go to law before *lay judges*, was not to go before unbelievers or unspiritual men. And further, St. Paul spoke to the laity, the people of Corinth; but the Church applied his principle only to the clergy. It was the clergy alone in the Middle Ages, who were regarded as constituting the saints, to whom the title of religious or spiritual belonged. The laity still belonged to the world, and were spoken of as *carnales*, carnal men, in contrast with the clergy, who were *spirituales*.

We have in these so-called spiritual courts, the germ of the papacy as a supreme court of appeals. For if each bishop was to hold his courts, and above the bishops' courts were the courts of the metropolitan or archbishop, it was necessary that the final appeal should be taken either to the king or to the Bishop of Rome. The kings, as we know, at a later time resisted the appeal to Rome. But the principle had been established by the forged decretals that the final appeal in all grave cases should go to Rome; and the sentiment of the clergy for the most part favored the practice of going to the spiritual head of the Church, as the surest means of redress in their troubles. Justice is not always an easy thing to secure in this world. It is not strange that the clergy, appreciating keenly the injustice of national tribunals, should have cherished the ideal of a justice which might be had beyond the sea, in the distant and larger world of the Bishop of Rome. It needed only that Rome should be given a fair opportunity to show the world its conception of justice, in order that so delusive a sentiment should forever disappear.

When Henry II. came to the throne in 1154, he was confronted with the difficulties springing from these ecclesiastical courts. The times in which he reigned were full of lawlessness, confusion, and misery; a strong king was needed, who could establish a powerful government and good order. Such a man was Henry II., possessing sagacity and courage and a legal judicial mind. The consolidation of the people into one nation, by which the distinction between Norman and English disappeared, is generally placed to his credit. In his reign an Englishman ascended the papal throne, Nicholas Breakspar, under the name of Adrian IV.,—the only Englishman who ever attained the honor. The connection between England and Rome became in consequence closer than it had been before. It is a circumstance which deserves to be recalled, that Pope Adrian made a grant of the schismatical country of Ireland to the English king—a circumstance which the generous hearts of our Irish brethren have never treasured up against the holy father. They are prepared rather to resent its acceptance by the king than its gift by the pope.

It was one of the projects of Henry II. to curb the power of the Church, which had been growing stronger in the kingdom since the days of Anselm, and which now threatened the rightful prerogatives of the king and the well-being of the State. With his inherent love of justice, the king was offended with the ecclesiastical courts in which the clergy took refuge, escaping the penalties which they would have suffered in the secular courts. In his attempts to bring the clergy to justice, he was opposed and thwarted by Thomas à Becket, who had formerly been his chancellor and his intimate friend, but who as Archbishop of Canterbury became his mortal foe. A bad case of clerical justice was the first occasion of the quarrel. A clerk by the name of Philip Brois had committed a murder and received no punishment. The civil courts had claimed to try the case and found him guilty; but Becket had insisted that he should be withdrawn from the secular jurisdiction, and had sentenced him to two years' deprival of his benefice. It was this incident which is said to have determined the king to restore the ancient customs of the country, when the clergy were amenable to the civil jurisdiction. At a great council held at Clarendon in 1164, what are known as the Clarendon Constitutions were enacted, which embodied the king's views,—what may be called the national view of the king's authority. According to the Clarendon Constitutions criminal cases among the clergy were to be determined in the king's court. Other laws were also enacted, such as that bishops should not leave the country without the king's consent, nor should they be allowed to excommunicate the king's men; and newly elected bishops were to swear fealty to the king.

These statutes Becket at first refused to sign; afterwards he signed them and then retracted his signature, appealing to the pope to absolve him for his sin in yielding. He now carried his case to Rome as Anselm had done before him; he took his stand upon the forged decretals in opposition to the law of the kingdom; he declared that he placed himself and the Church under the guardianship of the pope and of God. Leaving the kingdom, as Anselm had done, he remained abroad, resisting the king and vainly expecting aid from a pope who was too busy or too prudent to give him the support for which he asked.

It is unnecessary to repeat the familiar story of Thomas à Becket. He long continued to defy the king, and his actions were so irritating and exasperating as to drive the king into a frenzy which he could not control. Whether the king was responsible for his murder is doubtful. As the story goes, certain of the king's attendants, supposing, from his language, that he would be pleased to be rid of Becket altogether, assassinated the archbishop near the altar of Canterbury cathedral, on the eventful day, December 29, 1170. It depends somewhat on our sympathies, whether they are with Church or State, as to the estimate which we shall place on the fate of Thomas à Becket. By some, notably Mr. Froude, his death has been treated as a righteous punishment for his treachery to the highest interests of the nation; by others he has been regarded as a martyr dying in a holy cause. The distinguished historian, Mr. Freeman, who is entitled to speak with authority, thinks that the principle for which Becket died was not the authority of the pope over the Church, but some minor point growing out of his belief that the prerogatives of the See of Canterbury had been invaded, so that in reality he died in the interests of a national cause. It is certain that he carried with him the sympathy of the people in his opposition to the crown. It is possible that the confused and complicated situation may yet be so read as to reveal Becket in the light of a friend of the people, with the cause of the people as the issue for which he staked his life. In those days the people as a force in civil society as yet hardly existed. It may be that they were not wrong in rallying round the Archbishop of Canterbury as their hope against oppression—the only man in the kingdom who could defy the king.

But however this may be, the death of Becket did more for the cause of the Church against the State than his life would have done. He became the typical martyr in the popular estimation not only of England, but of Europe. In Becket England gave to western Christendom the most influential saint of the middle ages; no shrine in Europe was so rich or so attractive to the pilgrim as the shrine of Becket in the Canterbury cathedral; and so it remained until the age of the Reformation.

The murder of Becket was followed by the humiliation of the king. He had already suffered one humiliation while the archbishop was still living, when, kneeling before him, he had held his stirrup as he mounted his horse,—a token that the civil power recognized its inferiority to the ecclesiastical. When Becket was murdered the outcry in England and throughout Europe made Henry aware that he had lost his cause. Overcome by this sentiment he undertook a pilgrimage to Becket's tomb, and there submitted to the penance imposed upon him. A night and a day were spent in prayer and tears, imploring the intercession in heaven of him who had been his enemy on earth. The bitter fruit of this victory of the Church, it now remained for England to realize.

Hitherto the popes had refrained from interfering with the struggles in England which were subjecting the nation to its control. But when Innocent III. mounted the papal throne in 1198, he undertook the task which his predecessors had neglected. Disposing of all other affairs which might embarrass him, he turned his attention to England with the purpose of bringing that refractory kingdom into formal submission to the authority of Rome. The moment was a propitious one. King John had made himself obnoxious by his tyranny to the people, to the great barons, and also to the dignitaries of the Church. When Innocent proceeded, contrary to the customs of the English Church, to appoint Stephen Langton, his old friend, to be archbishop of Canterbury and the appointment was resisted by John, the pope issued the ban and interdict which freed the subjects of the king from their oath of allegiance, and forbade also the performance of Church services throughout the kingdom with the exception of baptism and extreme unction. In the year 1209 he excommunicated the king. For nearly two years John continued his opposition despite the action of the pope and his desertion by the clergy. But when France began to prepare an army for the purpose of invading the kingdom and driving him from his throne, the spirit of the man was overcome and he stooped to the lowest degradation. He resigned the crown of England and Ireland into the hands of the papal legate and received it back again as a gift of pure grace on the part of the pope, to be held henceforth as a papal fief on condition of the payment of an annual tribute of a thousand marks.

Such was the humiliation of England at the hands of the great Pope, Innocent III., who regarded himself as the sun shining by his own inherent light, while the kingdoms of Europe were regarded as satellites or planets shining with his reflected light. It was the custom of the popes to apply to themselves the large language of the inspired Psalms of David. A favorite passage was the language of the second Psalm: *The kings of the earth stand up and the rulers take counsel together against the Lord and against His anointed.* Hildebrand on his death-bed applied to himself the words: *I have loved righteousness and hated iniquity, therefore I die in exile.* The attendant priest encouraged him, "Thou canst not die in exile, vicar of Christ and His apostle; *thou hast the heathen for thine inheritance and the uttermos parts of the earth for thy possession.*" It was a favorite passage with Innocent the Great: *The righteous shall have dominion over them in the morning. Though thou hast lain among the pots, yet shalt thou be as the wings of a dove, which hath silver wings and her feathers like gold.*

A few years ago, in the pages of the *Nineteenth Century*, in which educated Englishmen carry on a sort of private conversation before the world, Cardinal Manning re-told the story of Innocent and King John, asking the English people, if it would not be for the interests of the nation to have such a fatherly adviser restored to his authority, who by his word could check disorder and misrule. But the Cardinal had forgotten the episode of *Magna Charta*, in which the oppressed and humiliated people asserted their rights—the charter of English liberties to our own day. Innocent had protested against the *Charter*, and done his utmost to prevent its acceptance. When the distinguished Cardinal was reminded of this circumstance, he replied that Pope Innocent had not probably read the charter and was ignorant of its real meaning and purpose.

It is one of the wonderful anomalies of human life, which may lend consolation in the hour of defeat and humiliation, that seeming victories sometimes promote the cause which ostensibly they have crushed. The conquest of the pope over the English nation was a crisis in its history from which date the movements that gave England the ultimate victory.

It only needed that the Church of Rome as embodied in the pope should achieve the end for which it labored in order that the falseness and untenability of its ambitious project should stand revealed. From this time on the interest of English history lies in tracing the steps by which the nation grew and the papacy declined. The impossibility of one man's ruling all the states of Europe became increasingly manifest. The papacy was a mischievous thing, because of its impossibility. We cannot see very far into the future, but one thing we can see, and should most devoutly believe, that God's will is that nationalities should be regarded as a sacred end in themselves. God has appointed that the peoples of the world should dwell in certain large families which we call nations. Here is an ultimate result in the divine purpose beyond which we cannot go.

There is a mystery about the birth and growth of a nation which we cannot always trace in the complicated process which it involves. It is true of states, as it is of individuals, that history seems careful of the national type, while careless of the individual nation. There are many attempts at achieving nationality and but few successes. The papacy had risen in Europe when nations were struggling to their birth or were still in the weakness of infancy. Everywhere the papacy stood for resistance to the growth of the national consciousness. The whole system of the Roman canon law, from the time of the forged decretals, conspired to hinder, to crush, if it were possible, the rising instinct which was urging the different peoples of Europe to the attainment of national independence. The question may arise what useful purpose, in a world where God is ruling, such an institution as the papacy may have subserved. It is best to be fair always in discussing such a question, for we gain nothing by sacrificing or obscuring the truth. Let us admit, then, that the papacy may have served some useful ends, in the divine economy. If it served no other purpose, it stood as a resisting force, against which the nations threw themselves, an obstacle which they must overcome, in order to their successful assertion of national existence. Purification of the national purpose, the clear consciousness of a divine call, must be reached by a struggle with such opposition as the papacy presented. But other ends were also served by the papacy. It held the nations together in their infancy by such close ties as to give them a common likeness and sympathy, a feeling of kinship which makes them a family of nations in the Kingdom of God. The striking difference in this respect between Europe and Asia has been often remarked. In Asia, the great kingdoms are separated by physical barriers and by other differences, such as religion, to such an extent that they have nothing in common. India and China are as distinct and widely apart as if they were in different hemispheres. But in despite of the differences which mark them, there is a spirit of community among the nations of Europe, which, though it cannot altogether prevent hostility and war, is yet a basis for the growth of the large sense of humanity—the promise of the ultimate unity of the family of God.

Whatever may have been the evils of the papal dominion—and they were great—yet individual popes were capable of disinterested action, and did not always abuse their power. The papacy served as a court of arbitration between monarchies and kingdoms, before any system of international law had arisen, or was yet possible. Those who still maintain, like Cardinal Manning, the usefulness and the necessity of the papacy, fasten their gaze upon circumstances like these, and feel that history is unjustly read when they are suppressed or overlooked. We, too, may then admit that the papacy has served a divine end. But even divine institutions may be removed by the same hand that has created them, in order to give place to institutions more fully charged with the divine will. So Judaism, which was divinely ordered, has given way to the Christian Church, while the Jew still remains unable to see that progress is the law, in the evolution and revelation of the will of God in the world.

From the moment when the papacy attained the fulness of its power, the great Protestant movement began, which called for reformation and ended finally in revolution. Great bishops and statesmen in the English Church, who were devoted to Rome and never thought of questioning its divine claim, appeared in protest against the evils it engendered all through the thirteenth and fourteenth centuries. Not only were things no better in England, after Innocent the Great had conquered the king,—they rapidly grew to be worse than they had been under the most tyrannical and irreligious of English sovereigns. Papal or religious investiture brought forth no better fruits than secular investiture. The Church was no better off when it was robbed by the papacy than when it was robbed by its own king. The difference was that the money now went out of the kingdom, when before it was used at home and indirectly enriched the people. The English Parliament complained in 1376 that five times as much money went out of the country to support the pope as the whole produce of the taxes which accrued to the king. The popes now claimed the ownership of all the benefices or property of the Church. Nowhere in Europe was the practice carried out to a greater extent than in England, by which the best livings and dignities were filled by the nominees of the pope.

In England it was almost like another foreign invasion, when Italian and Spanish and French priests were everywhere found in English monasteries as priors or abbots, in English canonries and English bishoprics. They did not understand the language of the people, they did not in many cases even deign to reside in England, but simply drew the revenues of their livings. If the kings had claimed gifts when they appointed high dignitaries, the popes claimed still greater gifts, until it almost impoverished a monastery or a bishopric when it was obliged to fill a vacancy. In this case it was a so-called *spiritual* power, professing to be above the temporal, which was weakening the Church no less than the State.

It may seem unworthy in itself that the great issues of Church and State—the supremest issues of human affairs should turn so largely on the question of money. But money is only the symbol of other things. Men are quick to see the large evils which its improper use creates. In the relations of life the highest qualities or the lowest of our nature are brought to light by the use or abuse of money. When a so-called spiritual power appears to be covetous of wealth, or eagerly concerned to find money for its schemes, it is degrading the entire ecclesiastical service of which it is the head, and it will not be long before the eyes of a people are opened to its hollowness and iniquity. Just as a partisan civil service is an evil corrupting the life of a nation, a debased ecclesiastical service undoes the spiritual vitality of the Church.

It was no doubt true that the papacy had need of all the money it could raise. As it grew in power and absorbed in itself the government of the Church and the world, it became a more and more costly thing to support. Self-government in Church or State is comparatively inexpensive. An absolute monarchy, such as the papacy really was, may become so expensive an object to maintain that at last it may break down from its inability to obtain the money needed for its support.

English legislation on the affairs of the Church from the thirteenth century onwards, shows a determination to go to the root of the question in regard to money. In 1279 the statute of *Mortmain* was enacted, which forbade the transfer of any landed property to the Church without the king's consent. What was given to the Church now began to be regarded as tending to the impoverishment of the nation. Again in 1343 there was passed the Statute of Provisors which prohibited the pope from appropriating the revenues of English benefices. When the aggrieved parties were found carrying their cases to Rome, it was enacted, in the Statute of Præmunire in 1352, that outlawry should be the penalty for carrying pleas to Rome, which belonged to the king's court. In the year 1379 an act was passed prohibiting the holding of benefices in England by foreigners. The Statute of Præmunire was again confirmed in 1392, and in 1404 the two statutes of Provisors and Præmunire were re-enacted, by which the pope was henceforth prevented from appointing to English bishoprics, and the king was forbidden to grant exceptions to the law.

But there was a deeper protest in the heart of the English nation than the desire to save the people from impoverishment. Great men arose, who saw with increasing clearness the ideal of what a Church should be. Such an one was Grosseteste, Bishop of Lincoln, who protested against the abuses caused by the presence of a foreign clergy, and was able to prevent Pope Innocent IV. from making his infant nephew a canon of Lincoln Cathedral. William of Occam, though he spent most of his life abroad, was an Englishman by birth and training,—a philosopher as well as a statesman, who broke down, by his vigorous incisive arguments, the vicious principles of the Scholastic philosophy, especially denouncing that metaphysical conception of the Church which exaggerated the importance of institutions, till it had made impossible the freedom and growth of the individual man. The famous Bradwardin, who became Archbishop of Canterbury in 1349, asserted the dependence of men upon God for their salvation, following Occam also in pointing away from the pope to Christ as the only real, though invisible Head of the Church. The "Vision of Piers the Ploughman," a book which had vast popularity and influence, exposes the evils which a corrupt official service was creating, sets forth in glowing terms the Christian ideal, and does not hesitate to recommend the remedy for the ills of the Church to its highest dignitaries. An evil life is for him an evil life, whether in pope, or bishop, or peasant.

And at last came Wycliffe in the fourteenth century, who may be regarded as the greatest man to whom the English Church has given birth in all her history. With a brief allusion to his work, I close my lecture. It is a remark of Milton, that "had it not been for the obstinate perverseness of our prelates against the divine and admirable spirit of Wycliffe, to suppress him as a schismatic and innovator, perhaps neither the Bohemian Huss and Jerome, no, nor the name of Luther and Calvin had ever been known. The glory of reforming all our neighbors had then been ours." I will not undertake to summarize his efforts for the reformation of the Church; how he resisted the pope, redefined the Christian doctrines, rejected abuses, declaimed against monks, translated the Scriptures, preached constantly, and sent forth preachers in his own spirit throughout the kingdom. He made mistakes, it is true; in his opposition to what was false, he may have gone to false extremes. But his errors may be forgiven to one who has done more for Christendom than any other Englishman.

And exactly what was it that he did, that made possible the overthrow of the papacy, and the emancipation of England from a foreign usurpation? I should answer that he laid down a higher doctrine of the relation of Church and State. He was the first to grasp the sacred principle of nationality, to implant in the consciousness of kings and people the idea of their divine and spiritual calling as a nation.

The kings of England and its archbishops, through the Norman period, had been laboring unconsciously for the great end which Wycliffe now unveiled in its majesty. But because they labored unconsciously, they labored often ineffectually or in vain. They were guided by an instinct which they were unable to formulate or define. But they builded better than they knew. Take the period we have been considering as a whole, and it reveals a progressive movement, even under weak or immoral kings, toward the same common goal. It is not a history which one need to be ashamed of or to apologize for. There was some latent divine element in the atmosphere of that little island beyond the seas, which gives to England a homogeneous principle through all its career. Hardly had the Norman kings landed in England, when the old process of the earlier history was resumed, and they began to work for a national end. Archbishops of Canterbury, even an Anselm, or a Becket, or a Stephen Langton, could not escape the subtle contagion of this mysterious motive. There are phases of their administration which may have a national bearing.

But the great deficiency of the period was the lack of an intelligible formula or doctrine, which would enable the nation to reject the false doctrine by which the popes built up their supremacy. When it was said that the Church was above the State, because the State dealt with temporal or secular concerns, the things that related to this earthly life, while the Church had the exclusive prerogative of dealing with spiritual or eternal interests, no one lifted up a voice in behalf of the State as having equally with the Church, a *spiritual origin, a spiritual purpose and a spiritual end.* Everywhere throughout Europe, men acquiesced in the common statements that only the Church was spiritual, and as such, must be placed above all earthly potentates. So long as they continued to think so, the power of the Roman popes was secure. What is the *spiritual*, when we ask for its definition? Is it not the *unseen*, the end not yet attained, the moral ideal to be achieved in the future, toward which the present is tending? *The things which are seen are temporal, the things which are not seen are spiritual or eternal.* The State then labors for the spiritual and moves toward it as by a divine decree. Wycliffe dared to hold up before the kings of England, a divine ideal which redeemed the nation from the degradation of inferiority and subjection to the Church.

But if the nation has a spiritual, divine character no less than the Church, where then lies the difference between them? Wycliffe's answer is clear and emphatic. The State represents the *dominion* of Christ, the power and rule of Christ in the world. If there must be a vicar of Christ, it is the king or ruler of the nation, not the head of the ecclesiastical principality. The State expresses and reveals the *dominium* or the power of Christ; the Church represents the *ministerium*, the service of Christ; as when Christ remarks: *I am among you as he that serveth.* The kingdoms of the world are the kingdoms of our Lord and of His Christ; their power is the power of Christ to whom is given all power in Heaven and earth. One function of the Church is to minister to the well-being of the State, in all the countless ways of *spiritual* ministration, of which Christ, who is still among us as one that serveth, is the type and illustration. It is the function of the Church to hold up constantly before the State its divine calling; in its prophetic office, to declare constantly and unhesitatingly the divine will.

Christ has a double character, one side of which is represented by the State, and the other by the Church. If either is higher than the other, it is the function of service,—the *ministerium*, as when it is said, *He that is chief among you, let him be as servant.* If the Church represents what is higher than the State, it is so because and in so far as the Church possesses faith in the spiritual purpose of the nation, even when the nation is without faith, —that faith which is the *substance of things hoped for, the evidence of things not seen.* But the condition of servantship still in this world implies a willingness to accept humiliation as its lot. Come what may, the State must have the authority. Priests and prophets have never known how to exercise power. The worst governments the world has seen have been administered by ecclesiastics. It is a mixture of things which are in their nature incongruous, when the prophet whose mission is to reveal a divine truth by moral insight, infringes upon the calling of the State and seeks to carry out his message by force. So long as the world continues must humiliation attend the *ministerium*, which waits upon the suffering Christ in humanity, when hungry, or naked, or sick, or in prison, or in the captivities of the human race, from which it seeks redemption.

This then was the work of the English Wycliffe, to place before his own countrymen and before the world the divine ideal of the State or nation. When it came to the Reformation of the sixteenth century, it is the cause of the *nations* against the *empire* of the pope. " The swing of the monarchy of Henry VIII.," as Canon Mozley has remarked, " was simply nationalism and nothing else,—the nation delighted in it."

The divine calling of the nations is as yet very far from being realized. But it has not hurt the nations to have proclaimed their true mission ; nor has it hurt or weakened the Church. The one thing which America most needs to-day is the reproclamation of Wycliffe's message. For there are those among us and notably also a foreign Church whose aim, whose necessity it is to rob the State of its spiritual prerogative in order to its own advancement. Here in this new world, the conflict of the ages is impending ; indeed, there are signs that the struggle has already begun. If our vision is clear, and as Churchmen we can follow Wycliffe in asserting the divine dominion of the State, the result cannot be doubtful. By our hesitancy or inaction the result may be retarded; but if the Word of God be true, it will only be a tarrying of the vision until the time be ripe for its fulfilment. In the book of the revelation of St. John the Divine, where the final glorifiaction of things is unveiled, it is not as Churches or as branches of the Church that the world stands at last before God, that humanity takes its rank in the temple and city of God. Into that city of which God is the light, the kings of the earth are represented as bringing their glory. *And they bring the honor and the glory of the nations into it.*

The Reformation Period.

LECTURE IV.

THE RT. REV. H. T. KINGDON, D.D.,
Bishop Coadjutor of Fredericton.

THE REFORMATION PERIOD.

THE Reformation of the Church of England was not the work of a few years, nor the result of any one force. It was the crisis of centuries of discontent, the irrepressible outburst of long pent up indignation, brought about by the resultant of many forces, religious, political, financial, domestic, civil. It took the form in England of a proleptic assertion of the Monroe doctrine, that no foreign interference could be tolerated in domestic matters. This feeling had always been very strong, and it so often showed itself where opportunity offered, that it may almost be said that the Reformation commenced from the time the Bishop of old Rome attempted to interfere in temporal and spiritual matters in England.

The first act of the English as a nation was to compel the acceptance of the Great Charter. This has been said to be " the first great public act of the nation after it realized its own identity: the consummation of the work for which unconsciously kings, prelates, and lawyers had been laboring for a century." The very first clause secured the freedom of the Church of England: " Quod Ecclesia Anglicana * libera sit, et habeat omnia jura sua integra et libertates suas illæsas." That the Church of England be free, and have all her rights undiminished, and her liberties unimpaired. From this we might say that the Reformation began with the signing of the Great Charter on June 15, A.D. 1215.

A century later the same feeling was evidenced in the Statute of Provisors (as it was called) passed in A.D. 1351, and of Præmunire passed two years later. The Bishop of Rome had claimed to suspend the right of presentation to benefices in England, in order that he might make *provision* for his own foreign adherents. Against this the Statute of Provisors was aimed ; while the Statute of Præmunire forbade appeals from the King's Courts, or obtaining bulls or other instruments from Rome, under penalty of forfeiture of goods, personal freedom, and protection of the law.

But these were mainly political, and did not touch the conscience so much as the terrible decay

---

* The title Ecclesia Anglicana, was anticipated in the correspondence of St. Thomas à Becket; where it is used interchangeably with Ecclesia Anglorum which had been used by Bede in the eighth century.

of vital religion and morality throughout Europe. From the beginning of the fifteenth century, there was one universal wail throughout Europe from holy men, deploring the state of religion, and laxity of morals. In Brown's *Fasciculus* is a list of works on the reformation of the Church. There are about one hundred such writers between A.D. 1400 and A.D. 1550. This would mean a great deal for a period commencing before the invention of printing, yet the list is not by any means exhaustive. I possess a little tract printed in 1489, " De Miseriis Curatorum," on the woes of parish priests, which is not enumerated in Brown's Catalogue. It seems to have been published in Saxony, as reference is made to Meissen in Saxony as a well-known wealthy benefice. The tract, consisting of fourteen pages, must have made some stir at the time, as at least three other editions were published. It is certainly valuable as exhibiting the state of things from the standpoint of a parish priest ; and we may learn from this why Saxony became so favorable to the views of the reformers. The writer says that the priests were worried beyond measure by " novem diaboli." I am sorry to say that one of the *diaboli* was the bishop himself. Another is the itinerant preacher, and the account given reminds one of the dialogue of Erasmus about the Franciscans, published about thirty years later. The Saxony priest complains of the exacting character of these preachers. "If you do not always give him the most delicate meats to eat and spiced wine with the best ale to drink, he will preach about it in the pulpit, and hold you up to scorn before the people." But the greatest wail is about one of the diaboli, which perhaps is the saddest of all: this is about the housekeeper or cook. In the midst of this the writer says: "There are three officials of the utmost necessity to mankind, the hangman, the knacker, the curate. The hangman strings up thieves on the gallows; the knacker removes dead horses; the curate teaches the people. The world cannot do without them; otherwise the thieves would seize everything; horses would become offensive; men would become brutal. But the more necessary they are to men, the more men despise them. There is no difference between them in the opinion of the laymen. Tell me, prithee, what virtuous, neat, chaste woman will ever be a servant to a hangman, a knacker, or a curate?" Thus on the continent of Western Europe there was a call for reformation.

The cry for reformation was equally earnest in England, and the English spirit revolted against foreign interference as well as against the means by which it was supported. England had long been regarded as a milch cow to yield *provision* for needy Italians who never visited England and spent their revenues in the Roman Court. For fifty years the See of Worcester was filled by a succession of Italians who spent most of their time and money away from England. Among them was Giulio de Medici, the bastard son of Giuliano, the brother of Lorenzo the Magnificent. This Giulio was afterwards pope under the title of Clement VII. At Salisbury, Cardinal Campeggio was bishop or was so called and drew all the income away, while he was really bishop of Bologna and never visited Salisbury. At the same time the dean of Salisbury was an Italian who never came near his cathedral and after twenty-four years was compelled to resign. These were *provided* by the pope. Can we wonder that complaints were continually made that the glorious cathedral of Salisbury was becoming ruinous? Such facts as these set going the financial force which tended to the Reformation. After much forbearance, the English revolted against their ecclesiastical revenues being spent to glorify the papal court.

Then there was the sickening adulation paid to the pope; as the Canonist complains, some sought by flattery to equal the popes with God Himself. Nay, in the Gloss on the Decretal there is the title "Nostrum Dominum Deum Papam," our Lord God the Pope, still printed certainly as late as 1609. This greatly moved such as knew of it in England, and is one of the things mentioned with abhorrence by Bishop Jewel. Still it does not seem much different from the claim reported to have been made by Pius IX. on the first of April, 1866. The French legitimist journal "Union," gave the text of his address in which he said: "I am the way, the truth and the life. They who are with me are with the Church; they who are not with me are out of the Church, they are out of the way, the truth and the life." It is a large claim.

Then there were the pretended miracles and miraculous images, the exposure of which caused a great shock to the devout minds of men. Henry VIII. was a firm believer in the Blood of Hales till nearly the end of his life. At Hales Abbey the pilgrim looked at a phial said to contain the Blood of the Saviour which was invisible to them in mortal sin. Some colored substance there was within glass of unequal thickness, and by turning the vessel half round, this was hidden or revealed at the option of the showman. Some of the more celebrated images were exhibited at Paul's Cross at sermon time, with the springs and levers by which they were worked. It seems hard to believe this, and yet somewhat of it is continued in our own day. A friend of mine, twenty-five years ago, was shown in Spain a fine white feather, which, said the priest, fell from the wing of the Angel Gabriel at the Annunciation. "Do you believe that?" enquired my friend. The priest took a pinch of snuff, and said: "Good for the people."

Can we wonder at the revolt against all this? Nay, we should rather wonder that the revolt came not earlier. It has been well pointed out that at the Council of Pisa in 1409, Constance in 1415 and just before the Council of Basle, English leaders had urged a reformation ; and for a long time, they waited for this to come from without. But it came not. It was like the fable of the lark and her nestlings. So long as the farmer waited for his neighbors to come to his help in harvest, the lark knew she was safe; directly the farmer determined to set to work himself, she flitted with her young. At length the English Church determined to reform herself; but how was this to be? There was the example set on the continent of Europe in various parts. At Pontresina on the Engadine, the population, inflamed by the earnest preaching of a Reformer, dismissed their priest, stripped their Church and flung all the furniture and ornaments, images, aye, and the sacred vessels into the river, and inaugurated a devoted personal worship of our Blessed Lord of which psalmody from the whole congregation formed the chief part. At Zurich, Zwingli disregarded the teaching of the Church, and sought to build up a body of doctrine from his private study of the Greek Testament.

No such scheme found favor in England. English people loved law and order; and all was done legally and in order. Everything was reformed by a careful examination of antiquity. It was, indeed, a passionate appeal to the primitive Church, so far as the practice and teaching of the earliest Church could be discovered. For this there had been much providential preparation.

The fall of the Greek empire was part of this preparation. Rome said that Constantinople fell because the Greeks did not symbolize with Rome. But in the Thirty-nine Articles, Constantinople is the only Patriarchate omitted from imputation of error, out of a tender consideration for their late distress.

The siege and destruction of Constantinople by the Turks had driven many learned Greeks to Western Europe; and their presence promoted the study of the Greek language and of the Greek Testament. The study was soon introduced into England, and without doubt helped on the Reformation there. John Colet, the eldest son of an eminent citizen of London, studied Greek in France and Italy, and returned to lecture on the Greek of S. Paul's Epistle at Oxford. Receiving preferment in London, he returned there, and soon was made Dean of S. Paul's. He at once began to preach on the Epistles in the Cathedral, and founded S. Paul's School for the express purpose of teaching the scholars Greek. This was in 1509. Boys to the number of one hundred and fifty and three, the number of the fish in the second miraculous draught of fishes, were to be taught there gratuitously. At the present moment six colonial Bishops owe their education to Dean Colet's munificence, myself among the number. Erasmus was a great friend of the Dean, and took great interest in the school. His dialogue "*pietas puerilis*" is supposed to show the excellence of the teaching given at that particular institution. All this helped on the Reformation. It was said by the monks that Erasmus laid the egg which Luther hatched. Certainly, his influence and teaching in England helped on the Reformation there in a conservative and healthy manner and direction.

The learned English at the time knew what they were about perfectly well, and we cannot think that they were left without guidance. For though we may and must acknowledge that in these troublous times, several leading English divines were somewhat rambling in their theology, feeling about as it were after the truth, yet in the authoritative formularies of the Church, there is no rambling, no error. Some years ago, one who might have been thought sufficiently learned in liturgical knowledge to have hesitated to impute error to others, said that the translators of our Liturgy were mistaken in one of their statements.

The statement which Mr. Seager objected to is "the ancient Fathers divided the psalms into seven portions, whereof every one is called a Nocturn." The translators were supposed to have misunderstood a lesson in the Breviary for S. James' Day. The Saint, it is said, "*Psalterium quoque per ferias distinxit, et unicuique feriæ nocturnum dedit.*" He divided the psalter for the days of the week, and appointed a Nocturn to each day. However, twenty years ago, the late learned librarian of the University of Cambridge, England, showed me a manuscript of the thirteenth century (I think). It was a commentary on the psalms appointed for each day of the week, and in this the division of psalms for each day is called a *Nocturn.* Thus the psalms for Tuesday are called the psalms of the third Nocturn. The translators knew what they were about, for they were familiar from constant use with details which we have to acquire feebly with long study. Nor did they make any statement or any change without laborious investigation. It was not without good reason that they challenged a condemnation of their work from the voice of antiquity. They had searched the ground, and were ready for the attack. Cranmer alone had a thousand folio pages of manuscript, quotations from the ancient Fathers, transcribed by his own hand in support of his views. Archbishop Parker had this copied for his own use, and this copy is now in the British Museum. Cranmer also transcribed much from the Scriptures, Fathers and Schoolmen before he attempted to formulate the Eleventh Article and the Homily on Salvation. This collection occupies seventeen pages of the octavo edition of his works, and this on the single question of Justification. He could, therefore, with confidence, write in the Homily, " Beside Hilary, Basil and St. Ambrose before rehearsed, we read the same in Origen, St. Chrysostom, St. Cyprian, St. Augustine, Prosper, Œcumenius, Photius, Bernardus, Anselm and many other authors, Greek and Latin." But Cranmer was not alone of this mind, as may be seen in any of the recognized formularies and documents of the Church. The Homilies lay down over and over again the principles on which Christian doctrine and practice were to be proved. " Ye have heard it proved, (i.) by God's word, (ii.) the doctors of the Church, (iii.) ecclesiastical histories, (iv.) reason and experience." Such is the universal statement, and the Homilies were to be "a pattern and boundary" for all preachers and teachers. In the Homilies, there are nine quotations from councils of the Church and two hundred and thirty-nine quotations from the Fathers. The four quoted most frequently are S. Augustine, fifty-nine times; S. Chrysostom, twenty-six times; S. Jerome, twenty-two times; S. Ambrose, fourteen. In Jewel's Apology, the councils are quoted thirty-two times while two hundred and seventeen citations are from the Fathers. Here again S. Augustine is the favorite, and heads the list with thirty-two quotations. Then Tertullian comes to the front with twenty-one references, and S. Chrysostom, S. Jerome and S. Ambrose come next in order. This is but a sample. The "general index" to the rather useless "Parker Society" books tells the same tale. Wherever the work of the Reformers of the Church of England is tested, the same principles are found to exist. The Reformation of the Church of England went on the plan of a passionate appeal to Scripture as interpreted by the ancient Fathers. "The primitive Church," say the Homilies, "is especially to be followed as most incorrupt and pure." The oft-quoted canon of 1571 maintains the principle, and enforces it on the clergy. "*Imprimis*, preachers shall take heed that they never teach anything to be religiously held and believed by the people, except that which is agreeable to the doctrine of the Old or New Testament, and what from that very doctrine the Catholic Fathers and ancient Bishops have gathered." Bishop Jewel professed, "We came as near as we possibly could to the Church of the Apostles, and of the old Catholic Bishops and Fathers; and have directed according to their customs and ordinances, not only our doctrine, but also the sacraments and the form of common prayer." " I prefer the antiquity of the primitive Church," said Bishop Ridley, "before the novelty of the Church of Rome."

Herein then was the essential difference between the Reformation of the Church of England, and the Reformation on the continent of Europe. The Church of England reformed herself, taking for her guide Holy Scripture as interpreted by the primitive Church; the continental reformers rather accepted the principle of Scripture, interpreted by private judgment. Private judgment is mentioned only once in the formularies of the Church of England, and then it is condemned. The Articles maintained that it is "the Church that has authority in controversies of faith"; and condemned those that "through their *private judgment* willingly and purposely break the traditions and ceremonies of the Church." But then the continuity and identity of the Church of England remained intact; she reformed herself. Her Bishops remained in the same sees, with their succession unbroken; whereas the continental reformers were compelled to break away from their Bishops, and inaugurate a plan of their own.

The "infamous Blackburn," as he has been called, saw this clearly when (in the middle of the last century) he wrote that the Reformers "determined the one (true) sense of Scripture to be the sense of the primitive Church, that is to say, the sense of the orthodox fathers for a certain number of centuries. From these they took their interpretations of Scripture, and upon these they formed their rule of faith and doctrine." As this was opposed to the unbounded liberty of private judgment, which Archdeacon Blackburn regarded as the essence of Protestantism, he thought that the Reformation of the Church of England was to be condemned. This testifies to the fact which meets us at every turn, that the Church of England in all things wills to be guided by Scripture as interpreted by the tradition of the primitive Church.

Here we must remember the perfect independence of the Church of England. Her very name shows her independence. In the eighth century Bede speaks of the Ecclesia Anglorum. In the twelfth century, in the correspondence of S. Thomas à Becket, we have both Ecclesia Anglorum and Ecclesia Anglicana; while from the time of the Great Charter in 1215, the name in Latin, Ecclesia Anglicana, has been the most frequent, though the phrase Angliæ Ecclesia occurs occasionally. She always had her own laws; and the Canon law of the continent of Europe never obtained in England except so far as the Church of England adopted and incorporated such canons as were regarded as suitable. This is so much the case that even now the Canons of Trent are not bind-ing even on the Roman obedience in England, because they have never been promulged and accepted there. The most striking instance of this is the marriage law. The law of the Church of England has always been that Holy Matrimony to be valid must be "*in facie Ecclesiæ, per verba de præsenti, per presbyterum sacris ordinibus constitutum.*" It must be celebrated openly in the Church by a priest in holy orders. This, the continuous law of the Church of England, was also the law of England until the middle of this century; but it was not the law of the continent of Western Europe. There mere consent before any witnesses constituted valid matrimony; it was the same as the present Scotch law which was anciently assimilated to that of France rather than that of England. But when, about the end of the sixteenth century and later, the Jesuits and other priests who had been trained abroad were sent into England to promote a schism, they knew nothing of the old law of the English Church, but brought with them the Canon law of the Continental Church before it was altered at Trent. There was no public authority in England to promulge the Tridentine Canons; these, therefore, were not of force. In consequence of this the law of marriage accepted at this day amongst those of the Roman obedience in England is perfectly different from the old law of the Church of

England, and would alone proclaim the Roman schism in England to be a modern intrusion.

Knowing this peculiarity of the Roman position in England, I had a curious conversation with a Jesuit priest in that country some years ago. At that time all Roman Catholic marriages were made valid in the eye of the law by the presence of the Civil Registrar, and my friend told me the following story: A nobleman was to be married, and there was to be pontifical high mass in the nobleman's private chapel. In the middle of the Creed, which was being sung, the Registrar came to the bridegroom and said, "My lord, I do not know how much longer this is going on, but it is five minutes of twelve, and if you are not married before twelve the marriage will be illegal." "What shall we do?" was the question. "Just step into the drawing-room with the bride, give your consent there and then return." This was done, and after the civil marriage in the drawing-room the couple returned into the chapel and the marriage service, which had been going on during their absence, still proceeded.

I at once saw I had the Jesuit priest on the horns of a dilemma. So I said, "Which of those was the sacrament of marriage?" He said, "They never told the bishop." "Never mind that," was my answer, "which ceremony was the sacrament?" "Of course," he replied, as he was bound, "the consent before the Registrar." "Then," said I, "the second consent was an iteration of the sacrament and sacrilege." "Ah, let me see," said the Jesuit, "before the Registrar they withheld their interior consent. I think that will do." "Then," was the reply, "the marriage is illegal as being after hours." "I think," said the other, "we had better talk no more about it."

This peculiarity of the Roman Catholic position in England is not generally known; the peculiarity of their law about marriage accounts for the stringent action of Cardinal Manning in preventing, or endeavoring to prevent, mixed marriages when the ceremony was often performed first in an English Church.

Having thus endeavored to exhibit the general principles on which the Church of England reformed herself. it will be useful now to see how these principles were applied in detail in some cases. Here we must be as brief as is consistent with accuracy so as not to exceed the limits of a lecture.

We must always remember that the Church of England has nothing to do with the private motives of Henry VIII., King of England. His public professions were excellent at all times, and the Church was only too glad of the opportunity afforded her to reform herself. If any one says that this king was not a moral man, the retort is ready that he was a saint by the side of the popes of his time. The heathen conceits of Leda and Europa, which are to be seen on the great bronze gates of S. Peter's to this day, are testimonies to the classical semi-heathenism of Leo X. Then the Borgia Pope Alexander VI., has no savory reputation. But it may well be said that these immoralities have not influenced for ill the Roman Communion. Still less have the peculiarities of Henry VIII. to do with the Church of England, of which he was no bishop. With respect to the position of the Church, in the matter of the Bishop of Rome, there was little difference between us and the true Gallican Church, until Napoleon the First conspired with the pope to destroy the Old Gallican Church by the stroke of a pen, and erect a new one on its ruins.

In declining to submit any longer to the Bishop of Old Rome, the Church of England was certainly following ancient precedent. As early as the beginning of the fifth century, the Church in Africa was troubled by the meddlesome interference of the Bishop of Rome, who claimed to hear and decide appeals under the pretended authority of the Council of Nicæa. Zosimus, Bishop of Rome, sent legates to Carthage, who quoted a canon as Nicene which was not to be found amongst the twenty canons in the text brought back from Nicæa by Cæcilianus, Bishop of Carthage, who had been present at the council. The legates of Rome naturally claimed that their copy was correct and the African copy was defective. The African bishops courteously agreed to accept the Roman text until such time as certified copies could be secured from Constantinople, Alexandria and Antioch. In answer to their request, Atticus, Patriarch of Constantinople, and S. Cyril, Patriarch of Alexandria, sent certified copies which agreed with the African, and disproved the Roman claim. It is hard to suppose that a Christian bishop would knowingly and wittingly falsify the code of Nicæa, and perchance his claim arose from ignorance. It has been suggested that the Sardican canons (which, indeed, were quoted), were written without any break after the Nicene canons, and that thus the mistake arose. But the illustrious Archbishop of Paris, Peter de Marca, in the middle of the seventeenth century, drily remarks, "the conjecture might be held to be probable, if borne out by the evidence of any ancient codex, but this has not yet been discovered." He thinks that Zosimus cannot be acquitted of wilful falsification. So early was the arrogance of Rome seeking to support itself on false claims.

Then with respect to one succession of orders, Bishop Jewel claims to have been ordained priest by the same bishop and the same ordinal as his opponent Harding, and then continues: "I am a bishop, and that by the free and canonical election of the whole chapter of Salisbury, assembled solemnly for that purpose. Our bishops are made in form and order, as they have been ever, by free election of the chapter; by consecration of the archbishop and other three bishops, and by admission of the prince. Therefore, we neither have bishops without Church nor Church without bishops." "To be short we succeed the bishops that have been before our days. We are elected, consecrated, confirmed, admitted as they were." Here, then, comes in another instance of the great care taken to adhere to precedent of antiquity. The confirmation of the election of Archbishop Parker was carefully framed on the old form used in the confirmation of Archbishop Chichell, in A.D. 1414. The form then used can not be traced earlier. "Its use was exceptional, having been resorted to at a time when the English Church did not acknowledge either of the rival claimants of the papacy. The tradition of that confirmation was only a century old. It was of the providence of God that they had that precedent to fall back upon. But the selection of this one precedent shows how careful Parker and his consecrators were to follow the ancient precedents." There was no particular of carelessness or haste about the matter. There was but one matter overlooked, but it was of no spiritual consequence. When Bishop Horne, of Winchester, tendered the oath of supremacy to Bishop Bonner (he being at the time in the Marshalsea, and consequently in the diocese of Winchester), Bishop Bonner took two legal exceptions to Bishop Horne's position. Had he known any more valid objection, he would not have confined himself to legal technicalities. First, Bishop Horne had not been consecrated by an ordinal which had statutable authority; secondly, Archbishop Parker had been consecrated by four bishops, three of whom had been deprived, and the fourth deposed by Act of Parliament. The ordinal used had been deprived of the authority of Parliament under Philip and Mary, but the act could not give or take away spiritual validity from the service. It was but a legal quibble, which was soon set straight by an Act of Parliament. Of the consecrators of Archbishop Parker, Coverdale was spiritually the diocesan of Exeter, though another had been intruded into his see; Hodgkin was a diocesan suffragan, the other two were "vacant" bishops elect to sees in the province. But then of Pole's seven consecrators, two were diocesan bishops, three were intruders, and two acting diocesan. Those who wish to pursue this particular branch of the subject should consult the accurate and precise little work of my friend and brother, John

Walter Lea, on "The Succession of Spiritual Jurisdiction." He gives the particulars of each see during the whole period of the Reformation troubles. It was most providential that Cardinal Pole, of Canterbury, died within twenty-four hours of Queen Mary; and within two years after the accession of Elizabeth, no less than fifteen sees were vacated by death. If Elizabeth did cause some Bishops to be intruded into sees not canonically vacant, her sister Mary had been previously equally high-handed and had intruded a similar number. But in neither case would this affect the validity of the succession. For such bishops would consecrate validly to the Episcopate, but invalidly to the particular see.

Mr. Lea writes: "Some of the results of this inquiry were unexpectedly satisfactory. I was not prepared to find the breaches in jurisdiction so few in themselves, so temporary in their consequences, and so evenly divided between Rome and England." "As to the duration of the Reformation disturbance, it was twenty-five years and less than one month; and canonical succession in every diocese was completely re-established by the consecration of Scambler's successor on February 7th, 1584-5." "On the whole I think we may conclude that the Reformation dislocation of succession [of jurisdiction] in the English Church has been greatly exaggerated by popular traditions and misconceptions. All traces, however, have long since disappeared."

Let us now turn to the question of the vernacular service. Several times have I heard the question asked by an enthusiastic ignoramus: " By what right were the services translated out of Latin into English?" The answer is so near to hand that it is difficult to understand how the question could be raised. " By the same right that they were translated out of Greek into Latin." Greek was the original language of Christianity even in Rome itself, and the first Christian Latin appears in the colony of Africa.

Two points have here to be touched upon: first, the adoption of one use throughout the Church of England and next the translation of that use into the vernacular.

For we must remember that there were several different service books in use in England, and each diocese adopted the variation which was most agreeable to the Cathedral. With substantial identity, these presented some inconsiderable variations; but they were all of the English Church. The Roman office books were *never* used in England until the Jesuits came in after the Reformation to create a schism. The first step of the English Bishops was to mould all the various uses into one. Thus the original preface to the one Service Book expressed it: " Whereas hitherto there hath been great diversity in saying and singing in Churches within this realm ; some following Salisbury use, some Hereford use, some the use of Bangor, some of York, some of Lincoln ; now from henceforth all the whole realm shall have but one use." This use, therefore, on the general title-page is called, " the use of the Church of England."

It is somewhat remarkable that almost all the manuscripts of the old service books of the Sarum use date from about A.D. 1420. It would almost seem as if there were some move at that time to renovate if not to reform the services. A century later in 1516, there is an unmistakable evidence of a steady design to amend the existing service books; and eighteen years later in 1534, the issue of printed service books in England, "suddenly ceased, and in the case of the Missal was never resumed up to the first Revision of the offices in 1549." Seven years later again by a regular Act of Convocation, the ancient and illustrious use of Sarum was extended to the whole province of Canterbury. This was on March 3d, 1541, and was the last step before the book of 1549, which was made obligatory on both provinces.

This extension of one Use to the whole of England went hand in hand with a gradual desire to popularize the services of the Church and make them adapted for congregational use. There is evidence of a continual tendency to have such services as were held in the nave amongst the people in the vernacular, in the language that the people could understand. Not only were they taught the creed, the Lord's Prayer and the ten commandments in their own language, but from early times the Bidding the Bedes was in the vernacular. About twenty-five years ago I drew attention to a very interesting service in English preserved in a fine Sarum Breviary on a spare leaf just before the Kalendar which is in the middle dividing the Temporale from the Sanctorale. It is the opening of the fifty-first Psalm with an Antiphon to be used at the Sprinkling of Holy Water. This was always done in procession amongst the people. The manuscript is ascribed by experts to the middle of the fifteenth century about 1450. As it is set to music, it was clearly intended for public use and was no private peculiarity. It forms an important link in the chain of evidence which shows how gradual the Reformation was in England; and for how long a period there was a steady determination to have the Scriptures and the Service Books in English. In 1534 and again in 1536, Convocation petitioned for an authorized translation of the Bible, and the Epistles and Gospel of the Communion service were printed and circulated in English. Then came the next step.

In 1544, Henry VIII. started for France at the head of a large fleet, and he was anxious to gain friends abroad and at home. To this end he caused what has been called the "King's Book," the title of which was, "The Necessary Doctrine and Erudition for any Christian Man," to be translated into Latin for circulation abroad. He wished to show foreign princes that he and his realm were perfectly orthodox, and the translation is very free with a good deal of new matter introduced. This desire probably accounts for the Latin name, "Pia et *Catholica* Xtiani hominis institutio." On the title-page of a copy in the Library of Salisbury Cathedral, there is written in handwriting of the sixteenth century, "Libellus supplex ad Cæsaream Majestatem et principes electores Germaniæ." A humble pamphlet addressed to His Imperial Majesty and the prince-electors of Germany. This was doubtless the intention of the book, though it was no friend of Henry that added the *supplex*. One thing at once strikes the reader of this book, there is one passage of Greek introduced. Greek printing was very rare at that date; indeed the scribe held his own in Greek against the printer for a long time. Just as the early printed books have the initial capitals filled in by hand, so we find Latin printed books with gaps for the Greek to be filled in by hand. This Greek quotation is in one of the fresh paragraphs inserted in the translation, and it is from S. Chrysostom. This would imply that between May 29, 1543 and February, 1544, some one in authority had been reading S. Chrysostom's works.

At the same time in 1544 for use at home, there was issued what we now call the Litany, but was then called also "the procession in English." Remark it is a *procession* said or sung among the people like the sprinkling of holy water just spoken of; the Litany is here called "Common Prayer of Procession." At the end of this we find the Prayer of S. Chrysostom as we have it now, another hint that S. Chrysostom's works were being studied. About this time, too, we read in a letter from Cranmer to the king that the Archbishop had been engaged in translating other *processions*.

Next after the death of Henry there followed in 1548, "the Order of Communion" when all which was addressed to the people, or said by the people, was in English, and the rest still in Latin ; and the next year following the service book was issued, which is known to us under the title of the first book of Edward VI.

As we should expect from the principles which, as we have seen, actuated the Reformers in England, there was all along the determination to bring the Scriptures in English before the people. About the same time, therefore, the Bible and

Prayer Book were translated. The public reading of the Scriptures was so arranged that, in the daily service, which was now popularized that the people at large might be induced to attend, all the Old Testament, or most of it, should be read once through in the year, and the New Testament three times over. But here again antiquity was followed and Isaiah was read in Advent in the Dominical and Ferial cycle of lessons, and after that Genesis was commenced. It was the aim of the English Reformers to make the people acquainted with the Scriptures. In a very wonderful way they have succeeded. For, though in my own neighborhood where I am now resident, the Scriptures are not as well known as could be wished, yet our daily familiar language, and almost every page, or even column, of the daily journals, testify to the prevalence of a knowledge of the words and phrases of the English Bible.

Yes, the English Bible is a priceless gift of the English Church to the English-speaking race. It was translated by the English Church for the English people. I speak not of the modern revised version, which is in no sense the work of the English Church. I mean the Bible as represented in the Prayer Book psalter, and that which is commonly known as the authorized version. All Englishs-peaking Christians, whether they own the tender authority of the Church or not, owe her this vast debt, that she has given them their English Bible. The beauty of the translation may be realized if any one compares it with any other translation. To give one example. How could we bear to hear read as a lesson in Church such as the following, from the Douay version — the mother of Sisera, "looked out of a window and howled. She spoke from the dining-room."

There is one widely prevalent mistake in English which has arisen from a mistaken understanding of a phrase in the Communion Office, which is a testimony to its influence. It is, unfortunately, a very common vulgarism of the present day, to say "I will try *and* do this or that," instead of "I will try *to* do it." This can only come from misunderstanding the exhortation to communicants "to try and examine themselves." *Try* in the sense of *test* is now rare, and some clearly have thought the exhortation meant that people were to endeavor *and* examine themselves.

Here then we pass on to another point in which reform was eagerly demanded; and no wonder. It was no less than the restoration of the Cup to the laity and such of the clergy as were present but not actually celebrating. The Sacrament had been mutilated and truncated, and there was a loud demand for the restoration of a complete Sacrament. The feeling of the laity was so adverse to this denial of the cup that in England and in many places on the continent after the laymen had communicated in the one species, an unconsecrated cup was ministered to them to assist (it was said) in the act of deglutition; but it was really to content the people. True, the priests were told to inform the laity that the wine was unconsecrated; true, they knelt to receive the consecrated element and stood to receive the wine. But the mass of the unlearned most probably were left in ignorance; while the learned resented the mutilation. The formal denial of the Cup to all but the celebrant only dates from the Council of Constance in 1415, though the custom had arisen in many places several centuries before, and it had rightly and justly given rise to great searchings of heart.

There is in my possession a manuscript volume of sermons on the Sacrament of the Holy Eucharist. They were written by the Dominicans of Cologne in A.D. 1268, and bear internal evidence of the work of S. Thomas Aquinas who was lecturing at Cologne about that time. In these sermons three reasons are given for withholding the chalice from the laity. The first is that so precious a gift should have a chosen vessel, such as the priest, to receive it. The second, to avoid the irreverence from the multitudes that receive at the great feasts. The third, to forestall a remedy for error in faith lest the rude multitude should think that Christ is not present entire under either species. The Scripture proof is curious: under the second reason it is argued that when the Lord administered to the Apostles at the Last Supper, as there were but few of them, He gave them the Cup; whereas, when He fed the multitude in the wilderness, He gave them bread alone. The next sermon says that the Blood of Christ is received by the faithful in three ways, first, *sacramentally* and this by the priest alone; secondly, *intellectually* by the people under the species of bread. The Scripture proof of this is Job xxxix., 30: " The young of the eagle suck up blood." There seems to be a confusion here between the eagle and the fable of the pelican, for the argument runs, " The young of the eagle, that is, the children of the Church, drink the Blood, not from the Chalice, but directly from the very Body of Christ." In further illustration or proof, two more passages are quoted. Canticles, i., 14: "My beloved is to me like a cluster of grapes"; and Ps. i., 16: "With honey out of the strong rock should I have satisfied thee." The third way of receiving is *spiritually*, by pious meditation on the death of Christ. We cannot wonder that men were not satisfied with such arguments as these. There was the institution of Christ Himself. He would not have instituted the Sacrament under two kinds, if one alone were sufficient. He would not have laid such stress upon their *all* drinking, if one only were to receive. The argument of concomitance and all such were swept away as making the Word of God of none effect by mere human tradition; and, thank God, the Chalice is restored to the laity.

There is, it may be, a hint of the time when the Cup was withheld in the use of the plural in the XXVth Article. "The sacraments were not ordained of Christ to be gazed upon or carried about." The two elements were spoken of as two sacraments. In the first Prayer Book of Edward VI. we read, "as the priest ministereth the Sacrament of the Body so shall he minister the Sacrament of the Blood." Some thirty or more passages of a similar character may be found in the official documents or private writings of the period. A similar use seems to be suggested by S. Isidore, of Seville, at the beginning of the seventh century, who says "the sacraments are Baptism and Chrism, the Body and Blood of Christ." Just as in the West, there is a divorce between Baptism and Confirmation, so there was also a divorce and mutilation in the sacrament of the Eucharist. Then again, as when Confirmation was separated by an interval of time from Baptism, there was a symptom of it left in the use of oil, and with us in the sign of the cross which is really part of Confirmation; so, also to content the people, there was the cup of unconsecrated wine given, a symptom and relic of the time when the laity were communicated in the Chalice.

Here again is seen the eager desire to return to the practice of the primitive Church; that all things in this (as the Homily saith), " be in such wise done and ministered, as our Lord and Saviour did, and commanded to be done; as His holy Apostles used it; and the good fathers in the primitive Church frequented it." The Church in the United States may be felicitated on having restored to their service a beauty, which we of the Canadian Church have lost in common with our common mother, the Church of England.

The next point to which I would refer is the marriage of the clergy. No one can doubt that the proposition of the article is absolutely true, that the clergy are not forbidden *jure divino* to enter upon or to remain in the married state. This has ever been regarded as a matter of pure discipline varying with the different ages, and the necessities of the Church; varying also with the public opinion of Christian society. In the eleventh century in the Church at Milan, the archbishop and all the priests and deacons were married; and Milan was proverbial for the excellence of the clergy. In England there was never a vow of celibacy taken in the ordination service, as was the custom on the continent; and though in the twelfth century canons were passed forbidding the marriage of the clergy, we learn that they had no universal effect, for the clergy married as before. Indeed, more than one instance is known of a somewhat exaggerated protest against such canons, when the priest had more than one wife. One such, the Vicar of Mundeham, in A.D. 1225, exhibited a dispensation from the pope allowing him to retain two wives. It was not at all uncommon in England and Wales for priests to be married. Indeed, it is said that the wife of Archbishop Warham, the immediate predecessor of Cranmer, was recognized by his friends in society. We need look no further than to a long list of surnames, English and Scotch, to see that if there were canons against clerical marriage, they were disregarded. In English we have Pope, Clerk in all its spellings, Bishop, Dean, Cantor, Cancellor, Cannon, Parsons, Chaplin, Priest, Arcedeckne, Deacon, Vicars, and others. In Scotch, Mactaggart, son of a priest; Mac Nab, abbot's son, all tell the same tale. In refusing to condemn the marriage of the clergy, there was a return to primitive antiquity, most desirable, and most loudly demanded on all sides.

To return now, in conclusion, from particular details to general principles. The position taken up by the Church of England may be learned from the fact that there is no large treatise of positive doctrine formulated by her; the Thirty-nine

Articles are mainly negative. The difference between the first eight of the Articles and the rest will be at once remarked. Where the faith of the Church is repeated there are few negatives; where the Articles begin to deal with errors current at the time, the negations abound. This would show that the Church took the teaching as she found it, but warned her preachers against certain errors which were prevalent at the time. The Creeds are " the Confession of Faith " of the Church of England. The creeds are what "the Catholic Fathers and ancient Bishops have gathered" from the Scripture. Of these, therefore, Archbishop Parker and the bishops in 1559, said, "Such as do not believe these must not be reckoned amongst true Catholics." Qui istis non crediderint, inter veros Catholicos non sunt recipiendi. It may be true that "The Bible, and the Bible only, is the religion of Protestants." No such statement was ever made by the English Church. Whichever way we turn, the same principles are manifest from the first. In A.D. 1533, in an Act of Parliament, we read, "that nothing in the Act shall be interpreted as if the king and his subjects intended to decline or vary from the congregation of Christ's Church in anything concerning the very Articles of the Catholic Faith of Christendom." Nine years later, in another Act, it is declared expedient " to ordain and establish a certain form of pure and sincere teaching, agreeable to God's word and the true doctrine of the Catholic and Apostolical Church." The same is seen under Edward VI., whose council speak of the book of the "ministration of the sacraments well and sincerely set forth, according to the Scripture and the use of the primitive Church." From first to last the same passionate appeal is seen. In the thirtieth canon of 1603, it is declared that it was not "the purpose of the Church of England to forsake and reject the Churches of Italy, France, Spain, Germany, or any such like Churches in all things which they held and practised"; but the right is claimed to reform "in those particular points wherein they were fallen both from themselves in their ancient integrity, and from the Apostolic Churches which were their first founders." This was the aim which the Reformers set before them. They worked hard to achieve their object; and, considering their opportunities, their accuracy is remarkable. To give one instance. There is a quotation from S. Vincent of Lerins which is very often cited now as a test of Catholicity. It is quoted in this form: "quod semper, quod ubique, quod ab omnibus." It is said that it is first quoted in this order by Newman in the Oxford Tracts. I have not verified this, but, certainly, in the last fifty years it has been commonly quoted in this order. Now S. Vincent's work is not easily found, and, therefore, inaccuracy may be pardoned in second-hand citation. But S. Vincent reckoned universality of place in the foremost rank, and wrote "quod ubique, quod semper, quod ab omnibus"; and Cranmer cites him accurately: "Vincentius Lirinensis teacheth plainly that the canon of the Bible is perfect and sufficient of itself for the truth of the Catholic faith; and that the whole Church cannot make one article of the faith, although it may be taken as a necessary witness, for the receiving and establishing of the same, with these three conditions, that the thing which we would establish thereby hath been believed *in all places, ever, and of all men.*"

Matters of doctrine cannot well be dealt with here in the small compass of a lecture, therefore, in detail they have not been referred to; but the same principles held in respect to these as to matters of practice and discipline.

In the great upheaval of those troublous times, there may be many things which we cannot now in calm dispassionate criticism wholly approve. But we were not living then and cannot be impartial judges because we cannot always understand what was at stake. Looking on at a distance we may discern the dust of the struggle, but we cannot always distinguish the exact point over which the battle is fought. For example, at first sight it is difficult to see why Hooper was compelled to "wear a square cap albeit his head was round." But the distinction between the laity and the clergy was at stake. At the Universities and so elsewhere the square cap marked the theological and clerical faculties; the round cap was worn by the lay faculties, medicine, law and the like. It was the same fight as over the name *priest*. But this contest was more fully developed later. There is much evidence that in the earlier years of Elizabeth's reign, the changes interpreted by custom and previous usage were comparatively small. We cannot think that so few ecclesiastics would have abandoned their preferments if it were otherwise; for there is no reason for thinking that by far the greater mass of the lower clergy were unconscientious self-seekers.

The position may fairly be represented by the picture as seen in Shakespeare's plays. He probably represented the current religion of the great mass of the people. The result is that some believe him to have been of the purely Roman obedience; some claim him as an Anglican of our type; others think he cared not for distinction of religious belief. He represents the old Catholic religion modified and reformed from excesses and superstitions; or, as has been well said, "Christianity alike Scriptural, Catholic and Reformed."

The changes were gradual, and caused but little friction in many parts. At Salisbury, at the commencement of the sixteenth century, Bishop Langton made a statute that all prebendaries on their installation should pay for a new cope for the cathedral. In consequence of this ordinance, in 1591, the great Richard Hooker paid £3 6s. 8d. for his cope on his installation, though at that time the money probably went toward the repair of the fabric, which the Italian dean had left in so ruinous a condition. At the same cathedral, the Morrowmas Chapel becomes the Chapel of Morning Prayer, and the Morrowmas rents become the Morning Prayer rents.

The Homilies represent also a transitional state of opinions. The Apocrypha is "the infallible and undeniable Word of God." Orders and marriage are sacraments, though not such sacraments as Baptism and the Communion. All show the same—it was a reformation of the old, and not a revolution introducing something entirely new. It is no wonder that there was no breach in Communion with the Romanists for more than ten years after Elizabeth came to the throne. It is no wonder that we hear of the offer of the Pope to recognize the existing state of things if only his authority were recognized in England. But this could not be. The people had never liked the foreign influence, and would not tolerate its fresh introduction.

It is interesting to read the testimony of the

great traveller, Sir Edwyn Sandys, in 1599, to the view of the more sober-minded foreigners about our Reformation. He writes: "In their more sober moods sundry of them will acknowledge [England] to have been the only nation that took the right way of justifiable reformation, in comparison of others who have run headlong rather to a tumultuary innovation (so they conceive it): whereas that alternative which hath been in England was brought in with peaceable and orderly proceeding by general consent of the Prince and the whole Realm representatively assembled in solemn parliament, a great part of their own clergy according and conforming themselves unto it ; no Luther, no Calvin, the square of their faith; what public discussion and long deliberation did persuade them to be faulty, that taken away; the succession of bishops and vocation of ministers continued; the dignity and state of the clergy preserved ; the honour and solemnity of the service of God not abated ; the more ancient usages of the Church, not cancelled ; in sum no humour of affecting contrariety, but a charitable endeavour rather of conformity with the Church of Rome, in whatsoever they thought not gainsaying to the express law of God which is the only approvable way in all meet reformations."

Such, indeed, is the view of candid Romanists now as ever; and we may well close with this expression of opinion.

But the Lord is King, be the people never so impatient: He sitteth between the cherubims, be the earth never so unquiet. The work is God's—there must be some great future in store for us. Just as of old, the Hebrew Church was cradled in the Holy Land, shut in on all sides from much intercourse with foreigners and then trained and taught, until in the fulness of time the Jews were driven into all parts of the world taking with them the Old Testament Scriptures and the knowledge of God; even so with the English Church. Isolated within the four seas she has been trained for some great work for God, until she sees her children in every part of the world carrying the English Bible and the knowledge of the teaching of the English Church: witness the assembly at Lambeth last year of the 145 bishops from every part of the world.

Surely the providential character of the English Church is not for nothing. Surely as she seems on the one hand to have somewhat in common with the various Protestant bodies who love the Lord Jesus Christ in sincerity, and on the other to hold on to the Greek and Roman Communions, so we may hope that in our Communion a means of reunion of Christendom may be discovered.

All honor to the Church here in the States for the move in advancement of this which was made at the last General Convention. Let us be thankful that the Lambeth Conference was able to endorse that movement. And while we hope that the time may come when " the envy of Ephraim shall depart, and the adversaries of Judah shall be cut off : Ephraim shall not envy Judah, and Judah shall not vex Ephraim "; let us end with the prayer of the man of blameless life and great learning—Matthew Parker—Archbishop of Canterbury :

"THE LORD DEFEND HIS CHURCH: GOVERN IT WITH HIS HOLY SPIRIT AND BLESS THE SAME WITH ALL PROSPEROUS FELICITY. AMEN."

Adveniat regnum Tuum, Domine; fiat voluntas Tua.

The Puritan Reaction.

LECTURE V.

THE REV. THOS. F. GAILOR, S.T.B.,

Professor of Ecclesiastical History, University of the South, Sewanee, Tenn.

THE PURITAN REACTION.

An eminent scholar,[*] a Unitarian, in the Hibbert Lectures for 1883, has remarked that "to enumerate the English among the Reformed Churches which own a Genevan origin . . . is a procedure conspicuously unfaithful to historical fact. Lutheran, Calvinistic, perhaps even Zwinglian lines of influence upon the English Reformation may be traced without difficulty; but there was a native element stronger than any of these, which at once assimilated them and gave its own character to the result. . . . The Reformation in England followed no precedents and was obedient only to its own law of development."

This may be taken as the mature judgment of history.

What that "native element" would have accomplished in the way of ecclesiastical reform,

---

[*] Prof Beard.

without any of these "lines of influence," it were useless to conjecture. Certain it is that this foreign interference in the conduct of the affairs of the Church of England is largely, if not entirely responsible for the pain and misery and contention of her subsequent history, and, therefore, for the present divisions of Reformed Christendom. That very theory of absolute uniformity in outward observances which provoked dissension, was imported from Geneva. The first Prayer Book of Edward VI., which expresses the mind of the English Church, is far less restrictive than the second Prayer Book, which was put forth at the instance of the continental reformers. And the germ of the theory of clerical subscription, that bane of later times, was introduced by a letter from John Calvin to Somerset, in 1548,[*] in which the great master of Puritanism says: "There be two kinds of men who seditiously stir themselves against you and the realm—those who walk disorderly in the name of the Gospel, and those who are sunk in the old superstitions. Both these and those deserve to feel the sword of the Prince." "Let there be a form of doctrine received by all and taught by all. Let all your bishops and parish priests be bound by oath to maintain that; and admit none to office in the

---

[*] Dixon, II. 525.

Church who will not swear." And yet down to the reign of Elizabeth, the " native element " in England left the penalty of recusancy to spiritual censures.

Foreign associations and internal dissensions began together. It was the reign of Edward VI., " the seven years' rule of an infant—the protectorate of Somerset and the domination of Northumberland "—" a chaos," it has been called, " in the semblance of order "—which witnessed the first considerable immigration of continental reformers into England and the first organized separation from her ancient Church. In May, 1549, we find Peter Martyr, the Italian exile and zealous Calvinist, thundering disaffection in the University of Oxford; and the more learned Bucer counselling moderation at Cambridge, in the face of bitter ridicule from his fellow-countrymen. In 1550, the numerous foreigners of every shade of religious belief had to be permitted to set up their own place of worship in the metropolis, in order that, by the protection and limitation of the law, they might be prevented from falling into the extremes of fanaticism.* Over them was placed John Laski, the Polish Bishop, the fiery revolutionist of East Friesland, who gladly imported his own congregation and his theological controversies into the hospitable island. The same year saw the

---

* Dixon, III. 233 and 208.

rise of small communities of separatists in the eastern and southern, and more exposed parts of the kingdom whose teachings were an incongruous mixture of Calvinism and Pelagianism with Anabaptist license. These were the first Non-conformists. John Knox, the Scotch Priest, has the credit of sounding the first note of rebellion against the rubric requiring kneeling at the Holy Communion. He had come to England in 1551, fresh from the galleys, where his alliance with the murderers of Beatoun had sent him, and was self-confident, fierce and ruthless in the exercise of his genius for the utter overthrow of the ancient order. The name of John Hooper, Bishop of Gloucester, sometimes called the father of English Non-conformity, deserves more than a passing notice. As early as 1539 he had fled to Switzerland and there under the influence of Henry Bullinger he had become an enthusiastic convert to the Zwinglian doctrines. On his return to England in 1549 he was almost immediately nominated to the Bishopric of Gloucester, in spite of considerable opposition on account of his revolutionary tendencies; but when he came to be consecrated, absolutely refused to wear the Episcopal vestments prescribed in the Ordinal or to subscribe to Cranmer's articles of religion. His main argument against the vestments is illustrative of the mental attitude of his class. Vestments, he said, were used by the Aaronic

Priesthood because the truth of their Priesthood, *i. e.*, Christ, had not yet come. " Christ hung naked upon the cross," and " since His sacrifice the truth no longer needs veil or shadow." * Hooper at first preferred to go to prison rather then wear the vestments, but soon afterwards relented and was consecrated. Strange to say he lived to become a model of Episcopal intolerance. We find him in 1552 ruling his diocese with a strong hand, enforcing clerical subscription without mercy, determined in requiring uniformity of practice even beyond the Prayer Book, especially when it was in the direction of his own opinions. It may be that the prospect of so many dangerous errors convinced him of the necessity of strict law; or perhaps he began to believe, with so many other men who have been called to bear the responsibility of high office, that even a tyrannical control is better than unlimited license for the welfare of religion and government.

But there was no spirit in Edward's reign endowed with sufficient authority and courage to check the prevailing tendency to disunion. The King was the perpetual target of unwearied preachers. Cranmer groaned in the weak struggle between the contending parties. The King's sanction of the revised Prayer Book seemed to be the

* Dixon, III. 216 n.

beginning of the end, when the death of Edward and the accession of Mary drove the most advanced reformers into a five years' exile on the continent, where they had leisure, under the influence of Geneva, to nurse their hatred against Rome, and to organize a determined opposition to the wise and moderate position heretofore occupied by the English Church. In the year 1555 English congregations were established at Wesel, in the dominions of the Duke of Cleves, at Arrow in Switzerland, Embden, Zurich and Strasburg and Frankfort-on-the-Main. Among them were many who afterwards became prominent in the Church, as Edmund Grindal, Sandys, Horne and Jewell. Of these congregations Fuller says* "Embden was the richest for substance, Wesel the shortest for continuance, Arrow the slenderest for number; Strasburg of the most quiet temper. Zurich had the greatest scholars, and Frankfort the largest privileges." Fellowship in suffering was not sufficient to unite the exiles. A fierce and unseemly strife about the use of the Prayer Book arose in Frankfort, in which Whittingham, Knox and Coxe were the chief contestants. An apologetic account of it, written probably by Whittingham, then Dean of Durham, and published in 1575,† has come down to us, containing Knox's scornful and unfair description of the Book of Common Prayer, and

---

* VIII., 406. † Reprinted, 1846.

Calvin's famous judgment on the "Book of England" wherein he decides that "there are many tolerably foolish things in the Liturgy," and expresses his astonishment at "those men which so greatly delite in the leavings of Popish dregges." Knox was banished from the city on account of his book entitled "An Admonition to Christians," in which he compared the German Emperor to Nero. The book was brought to the notice of the magistrates by Knox's opponents, and they reluctantly admitted it to be treason and gave the victory to the ceremonial party. It is interesting to note that in all these contentions about the surplice and responsive worship Bishop Hooper's case was constantly referred to. The troubles at Frankfort mark the real beginning of Non-conformity. Hardly a man returned to England who was not determined on further reformation on Genevan lines. Many of the exiles, smarting under their injuries, actually burned with the desire to abolish the last remnant of connection with the old order. To them Lutheranism was not only a base compromise, but a gross hypocrisy. The Pope was the visible anti-christ and child of Hell.

The reign of Elizabeth is in many respects the most important as well as the most difficult to understand in English history. For at least thirty years Church and State together rocked and trembled between contending factions; and whatever faults of character or of policy may justly be charged against the Queen, it is to her immortal honor that she had the courage and the ability to achieve triumphant success in the face of almost unequalled difficulties. It is not accurate to attribute every thing to her. She was Henry's daughter, but she cannot be said, like him, to fill the whole canvas. She was intelligent enough to divine what the mass of her people wanted, and courageous enough to insist upon it. More than once she yielded her own will to that of parliament. More than once she found it necessary to modify her orders about religion. Had her conscience and her piety been equal to her intellectual grasp, she would have treated her Archbishops and their convictions with more consideration, and saved her successors many trials. As it was, she came to the throne in November, 1558, and at once adopted, with the advice of her ablest ministers, that conservative attitude in religion which we have come to honor as Anglo-Catholic. To this she was intellectually loyal to the very end, although she permitted her greatest court favorite to torment the Archbishop by open encouragement of both Puritan and Roman dissentients. There was practically no opposition to her conservative policy. As Mr. Gladstone showed last year,* the indefi-

---

* *Nineteenth Century*, July, 1888.

nite resolutions of the lower house of Convocation amounted to nothing. Mary's reign had cured England of Popery, and when subscription to the new order was demanded, only 192 out of more than 9,000 clergy refused ; and of these, only eighty were rectors of churches.* As Mr. Green says, at least two-thirds of her people were with her, among them the older and wealthier of the gentry of the kingdom, and no marked repugnance to the new worship was shown by the people at large. It took foreign influence, from Rome on the one side and Geneva on the other, to stir up the strife during the subsequent years of her reign, which occupies so much of the space of ordinary histories, that one almost wonders when he reads the one-sided account of innumerable grievances, whether there were any adherents of the established Church at all. Yet, the acts of this reign mark the practical conclusion of that readjustment of the doctrinal and liturgical system of the Church which we call the Reformation. The strong and clear assertion and maintenance of the Church's historical continuity, were agreeable to the nation, and were destined to survive. The miserable Nag's Head fable is now universally discredited.† The insertion of the Ornaments Rubric; the rejection of the title "Supreme Head"; the limitation of the test of heresy to Holy Scripture,

---

* Strype. Annals. I. 106 ; Heylin II. 295.
† Cf. Hibbert Lectures, 1883.

and the first four general councils; the public declaration of the venerable antiquity and independence of the English Church—these are facts with which we are all familiar.

The return of the exiles in 1559, marks the beginning of Puritanism, although that name does not appear until about five years afterwards,[*] and then has no invariable signification. There were men in Elizabeth's reign, called Puritans on account of their strict lives, who were loyal Churchmen, but the effort to shift the name was not successful. The later Puritanism was a thing of gradual growth, and there were always various shades of opinion included in the designation. There were doubtless some quiet souls who conformed to the established usages of the Church, and who would have been better pleased if certain ceremonies had been omitted. Others refused to conform to the wearing of the surplice, kneeling at the Holy Communion, and using the sign of the cross in Baptism, but did not attack the ecclesiastical government. And finally, the true Puritans, led by Cartwright, fought for the abolition of the Church of England, and the substitution of what came to be known as Presbyterianism, without thought of toleration in any direction.

Calvin naturally undertook to give directions as

---

[*] Fuller, IX. 474.

to the proper method of reform in England, but his letter was disregarded.* The more prominent of the exiles began, on their return, an ineffectual movement to do away with the compulsory use of the surplice and academic habit. Some of them became Bishops, and all of them manifest in their letters a great horror of Lutherans, Anabaptists, Arians, and other heretics (not Calvinistic), and this very dread of heretics evidently chilled their ardor for changes when they realized the possible outcome of the Puritan movement. In 1567, we find in the Zurich letters, two of these bishops writing to Bullinger and Gualter, in great disgust at the crudeness and violence of the Puritan faction. Nine years afterwards, in a letter to Gualter, they thanked God for the enforced silence of those " contentious, vainglorious, mischievous men, who with ungovernable zeal for discord, led the people into a madness of error, called purity."†

It was well for the Church that a man like Matthew Parker was Archbishop of Canterbury. He has been rightly called "the great conservative spirit of the English Reformation." His ripe learning, especially in ecclesiastical history and antiquities, made him a primitive and Catholic Churchman, whose influence upon Elizabeth in her earlier years may in some measure account for her

---

* Ep., p. 133, Heylin. † I. 177.

own predilections. His zeal for learning and his preservation of manuscripts have won for him an honorable name among all historians; and his wisdom and firmness in dealing with the two fanatical extremes he was compelled to cope with, gained for him enemies, some of whom rebelled against his authority, and confessed after his death that he was "a godly man with a zeal for true religion." His visitation in 1564 revealed so much disorder and irregularity in the performance of public worship—and the Queen herself had accidentally witnessed such shameful sacrilege—that by her order he consulted with the Bishops of the ecclesiastical commission and proceeded to enforce the law. While Neale, the Puritan historian, regards the "Popish vestments" as the original sole ground of dispute, there was evidently a determination to increase the demand. Humphreys and Sampson in 1566 wrote[*] to their advisers in Zurich and Geneva complaining of the cap and surplice; the use of music and organs; sponsors and the cross in Baptism; kneeling at the sacrament and the use of unleavened bread, besides the removal of the explanatory rubric at the end of the communion service. Bullinger's advice to them was learned and moderate, but Beza was fierce and sweeping. The new-made Superintendents in Scotland finally expressed their opinion in a letter

---

[*] I. 164.

"breathing," as Neale says, "an excellent spirit," in which they say "if surplice, corner-cap and tippet have been badges of idolatry, what have preachers to do with the dregs of the Roman beast." * An argument quite convincing to men who said that according to Jerome "gold that was ordered for use in the Jewish Temple could not be used for ornament in the Christian Church, and so much less can copes brought in by Papists be used in Christian worship."

The Puritan leaders were vigilant, aggressive and determined, and they lost no opportunity for the propagation of their opinions, and open ridicule of the law. The Archbishop resorted to severer measures. The more active and turbulent were deprived, and as Puritanism was not so much a popular as a clerical party, this step threatened serious injury to their cause. They resorted, as Neale says, to that door of entrance to the ministry which was providentially left open to them.† For by bull of Alexander VI. the University of Cambridge was authorized to license twelve preachers each year independently of the Bishops, whose authority it was ever the Papal policy to depreciate; and now this privilege the Head of the University made use of for the relief of the Puritans, not without a protest from the Archbishop, and the scorn of some who

---

* I. 95. † Ibid, I. 101.

despised this alliance between "their Herod and their Pilate." The year closed with a flood of pamphlets and sermons, and in midsummer, 1566, some of the deprived ministers finally separated from the English Church, and set up a new worship with the Genevan service-book, and without the "idolatrous gear of the Papists." Four years afterward the adherents of the Pope also formed separate congregations in consequence of the bull of Pius V., excommunicating the Queen and absolving her subjects from their allegiance. The rest of Parker's life was a struggle to preserve the order and existence of the Church in the midst of various sects, which took courage from these two beginnings of organized dissent and logically asserted their equal right to live. It is curious to read the plea of the Puritan historian * for individual liberty in the interpretation of Scripture along with his fierce and contemptuous description of Quietists, Brownists and Anabaptists. They were perilous and trying times for Parker and his coadjutors. The Bishops were urged in some cases against their better judgment to adopt extreme measures, and in official documents were accused of lukewarmness† and neglect of their spiritual duties, while at the very time they knew that the Non-conformists were

---

* Neale, I. 151.   † Cardwell's Annals, I. 385.

secretly encouraged by the unscrupulous Leicester, and other powerful members of the royal council. In 1573 Parker warned the court that the end of this movement was the overthrow of civil government, but it was not until 1592 that the Privy Council had courage to declare with the Bishops, that for the Church to attempt to satisfy the demands of every sect that arose, would be to put a premium on disputations and disunion. Parliament was beseiged with bills and petitions for further reforms in the direction of the Genevan discipline. The petitioners drew up no less than three revised and expurgated Prayer Books, one after another,* and the more they purified the less satisfied they seemed to be with it. The godly zeal ran into fanaticism, and fanaticism rapidly became crime. Puritan preachers strove to awe the multitude by the display of miraculous power,† and devils were cast out of some poor creatures, who afterwards confessed that they had duped the crowd. Mr. Hatton, a member of the Council and afterward Lord Chancellor, was finally singled out for assassination by a Puritan zealot, who said he was "moved by the Spirit of God to kill him as an enemy of God's Word, and a maintainer of Papistry." Parker died in 1575. He had left his mark for good. No historian questions his fitness

---

* Strype's Whitg. II. 340.   † Fuller, III. 78.

in moral character and intellectual ability for his high office, but some have condemned him for his efforts to enforce obedience to the law. His own letters are the best evidence of his moderation, his desire for peace, his humility, his deep distress at the opposition and discouragement met with in the performance of what he knew to be his duty. It was not natural that the Puritans should love the man who had effectually opposed them. In the next century when they came into power they tore the Archbishop's body from its grave, sold the lead of the coffin, and buried the remains in a dung-hill. Edmund Grindal succeeded to the primacy. He had been an exile in Mary's reign, and was known to favor the more moderate Puritans. His one year of office is only memorable for his encouragement of a Puritan practice of public disputation among the clergy and laity called "Prophesyings," which bred mischief and strife throughout the country. He had the courage to resent the Queen's arbitrary interference and was suspended for contumacy, although he was afterwards restored and died in possession of his see in 1583. His successor, John Whitgift was a man of different mould, a Churchman after the type of Parker, and his vigorous administration was destined to bring about a new order of things in quieter and less tumultuous times. Whitgift was a man of learning, keenly alive to the importance of the questions of the hour, and he entered upon the discharge of his duties with decision of character and manliness of conviction.* His boldness and courage in the defence of the Church rallied round him many dispirited Churchmen, and opened the eyes of all to the insidious and volcanic agencies by which they were surrounded. Hitherto Churchmen had been cautious, conservative and defensive in their arguments. The boldness and aggressiveness had been largely with the Puritans. And it was true then, as it is now, that the side which was thrown on the defensive, which dared not to assert itself, was losing ground. The remarkable revival of the English Church towards the close of the century was due under God to the confidence and vigor with which Whitgift and his colleagues, casting off the yoke of the modern reformers, and planting themselves upon the early Church, attacked and exposed the positions of their opponents. There was indeed an aspect of severity in the firmness with which the law was enforced. The Court of High Commission was freely used. Clerical subscription to the Prayer Book and the articles was insisted on. Prophesyings were put down. Irregularities and flagrant violation of the rubrics were conscientiously punished, and the government of the Church was as-

---

* Hardwick Hist. of Ref., p. 237.

serted independently of the patronage of the Swiss authorities, as being of Scriptural and divine authority. The younger men in the Church began to realize that here was something worth fighting for: that the Church of England not only had a right to exist, but the very best right to exist— that she was not simply to be tolerated by the modern founders of the only true religion, but that she had her own ancient title-deed in the Scriptures themselves and the Christian history of fifteen centuries. This saved the English Church from the Puritans' "Holy Discipline." This assertion of her historical continuity, of her lawful inheritance from the ancient Church became the rallying ground of earnest men, and saved her from complete destruction at the most critical period in her history.

The advance of Puritanism in influence and numbers during the first twenty-five years of Elizabeth's reign, may be easily accounted for if we remember the condition of the times. Europe was a seething sea of discord. That cold and brutal inquisitor, the Duke of Alva, was just beginning, with his "council of blood," the reign of terror in the Netherlands which led to the heroic struggle and assassination of William of Orange in 1584. The civil wars in France had reached their climax when Catherine de Medici and the Guises, not without the Pope's approval, had horrified Europe with the massacre of St. Bartholomew in 1572. Spain, suspecting England's interference in the affairs of Holland, was encouraging treason in England and Ireland, and was making preparations for an irresistible and overwhelming invasion. It is impossible for us to realize the conflicting doubts and fears of Englishmen in the presence of so many dangers. The Queen, excommunicated, deposed, declared to be a usurper, and her subjects incited to rebellion by one who had been but a few years before the spiritual head of Christendom, and who had now the richest and most powerful king in Europe pledged by religion and by personal interest to execute his orders; Ireland on the west in a state of utter lawlessness and misrule; Scotland on the north boiling with civil and religious discord; a rebellion of the Papal party in the North of England under one of the most powerful of the nobles; and Mary of Scotland, with all her pitiful history, the heir to the crown, a Roman Catholic, leagued with Philip of Spain for the overthrow of the government, and conducting her intrigues with more or less voluntary treason under the very shadow of the throne. These were the times when the world was divided by the sword of extermination into Papalists and anti-Papalists; when Churchmen thanked God even for Calvin's form of Protestantism; when the Church of England was compelled to recognize the Continental Churches of every type in some way, as sisters in distress, and gladly sent of her money and sympathy to the aid of the Genevan reformers, even when they had denounced her government and ceremonies. Perplexed by the terrors of the time, men, even like Parker, faltered and hesitated in asserting the Church's claims; and the leaders of the Puritans, taking courage from that hesitation, roused to a very ferocity of zeal against Popery, became more and more rampant in their demands for further changes. The Jesuits took advantage of this internal dissension, and sent their emissaries to play the part of Puritans. In 1569, a paper was found on an arrested Jesuit, in which three men, Hollingham, Coleman, and Benson, are mentioned as being employed "to sow faction among the heretics," and these very men are unsuspectingly described by Fuller and Heylin as violent Puritans.*

Thomas Cartwright is called by Neale the "Father of the Puritans." His public career began at Cambridge, where he was Margaret Professor of Divinity in 1572, soon after the publication of the famous "Admonition to Parliament," in which, among denunciations of the Prayer Book and Prelacy, a brand-new Church is recommended, whose holy discipline should copy the

---

* Curteis, B. L., p. 63 n.

Presbyterian models extant in Scotland and Geneva.* Cartwright defended the Admonition in a controversy with Whitgift, which extended over a period of about four years, and in which he established his reputation for unparalleled self-confidence and insolent fanaticism. Mr. Green says,† that "his bigotry was that of a mediæval inquisitor." To him, the rule of Bishops was begotten of the devil; but the rule of Presbyters was established by the Word of God. This was a new departure. For, according to Neale, the moderate Puritans in 1571 would have been satisfied with mild concessions. They would use the Prayer Book, provided that they did not kneel at the Holy Communion; that there were no organs nor singing; that no one was allowed to walk abroad, or sit idly in the streets during service time; that ministers examined into the private lives of communicants; that children were instructed in Calvin's catechism—and other matters of this sort.‡ But Cartwright was bent on revolution. The language of the "Admonition" was, "The Bishops are a remnant of Anti-Christ's brood, which do battle to Christ and His Church, and I protest before the eternal God I take them so." The ceremonies one and all were the intolerable marks of the Roman beast. The Calvinistic or Presbyterian scheme of government was exclusively, absolutely, divinely

---

* Hardwick, p. 236.   † p. 468.   ‡ I., 117.

true, and the ministers so ordained were not only the arbiters of religious doctrine and discipline, but the guardians of public morals. The State must be subject to the Church, and that the Calvinistic model. The penalty of all heresy was death. "I deny," wrote Cartwright in 1573, "that upon repentance there ought to follow any pardon of death. Heretics ought to be put to death now. If this be bloody and extreme, I am contented to be so counted with the Holy Ghost.' * But Cartwright's utterances were mild compared with the "Martin Marprelate" tracts, which began to appear early in 1588. These documents are marvels of vituperation and scurrility, even for that age. It would be painful to quote the language. The Puritan historian describes them† as "bitter, rude, and unbecoming," and regrets that "controversy about serious things should run such dregs."

Thus Presbyterian Puritanism reached its high water mark in 1590, and as soon as its ultimate aims became generally recognized, its influence began to wane. Several causes contributed to bring about this change. First, the aspect of the political world was far more encouraging, and England was no longer disturbed by internal discord, or the threat of foreign invasion. The civil wars in France had ended with the accession of a Protestant king, who conformed, from mo-

---

* Green, 469. † I. 189.

tives of policy, to the Roman Church, but tolerated his former colleagues. The mighty Spanish Armada had foamed itself away in the English Channel; and the unhappy Mary Queen of Scots, had expiated all her crimes upon the scaffold. England was at peace, and a native literature, unequalled in the world, had burst into splendid flower. The intellect of Germany was still exhausted by theological debate. The noble literary promise of Italy and Spain was crushed by civil and religious despotism Shakespeare, the glory of modern letters, was the child of conservative and Catholic England. Second, and above all, the Church herself was represented by a new generation of scholars, who had learned to love her doctrine and her worship, and were not afraid to throw off the influence of the continental reformers, and boldly to defend her on the solid grounds of Scripture and of history. Bancroft openly proclaimed the doctrine of the Apostolical succession in his famous sermon at St. Paul's Cross in February, 1589, and it was warmly defended by a learned layman of the Queen's Chamber the same year. Twelve months afterwards Saravia's book asserted the same doctrine, and Bilson followed in 1593 with his " Perpetual Government of the Church." Hooker's crushing reply to the Puritans, in his " Ecclesiastical Polity " finally appeared in 1594. One more attempt to Calvinize the Church by the adoption of the Lambeth Articles, was made in 1595, and was at first approved by Whitgift, whose theological learning was largely drawn from modern Protestant sources. But the time for such an alliance was passed. Men like Andrews, Overall and Harsnet, opened the eyes of the Archbishop, who had long since learned to doubt the infallibility of Calvin and Beza, and the scheme failed. This was practically the end of dissenting Puritanism as a religious movement, since the Presbyterian theory, as Green says, never had any general hold on England, for, even in the moment of its seeming triumph under the commonwealth, it was rejected by the vast majority of the people. The close of Elizabeth's reign was marked by a steady, healthy development of loyal Churchmanship, which had certainly vindicated itself in the face of the two great extremes of theological antagonism, and was about to enter upon a new trial, in which unhappy political complications well-nigh accomplished its destruction. Some of the most prominent of the Puritans realized themselves that a reaction had set in. We have already seen how Hooper, the first Non-Conformist, lived long enough to appreciate the dangers of indiscriminate license in matters of discipline, and became at last a strict and unflinching promoter of uniformity in his diocese. So also Robert Brown, the founder of the Independents, or Congregationalists, the most logical, but not least intolerant branch of the Puritans, who has been immortalized by the migration of some of his followers to New England in the Mayflower and by the triumph of his sect under Cromwell, became wearied with the discords which he himself had fostered. His separatist communion in Holland was rent with internal strife, and Brown had to retreat to Scotland and thence to England, where, by the influence of his kinsman, Lord Burleigh, he was allowed to make his peace with the Church and die in her communion. And Thomas Cartwright, the pitiless iconoclast, whose language failed him in the expression of his disgust at Prelacy, was conquered at last by the forbearance of Whitgift* and the prospect of contending sects. He died in 1601 in friendly submission to the Church's authority, expressing upon his death bed † " his sorrow for the unnecessary troubles he had caused the Church by the schism he had been the great fomenter of, and his wish that he might begin his life again in order that he might testify to the world the dislike he had of his former ways."

The reign of James I. marks the beginning of a new era. We are all familiar with that character which the genius of so many historians has portrayed. The King was indeed insignificant in his

---
* Fuller, 163.   † Strype, Whitgift, II. 460.

appearance; narrow and petulant in his humors; childishly vain of his superficial acquirements and fatuously jealous of his royal prerogative, but with all this not incapable at times of the display of much shrewd common sense and a rather caustic wit. His stormy experience in Scotland had thoroughly cured him of Puritanism, and his association with the great English Divines of the day made him an intelligent and ardent Churchman. The Church and the Crown were heartily united, not only on the ground of State policy but also of religious conviction. We all know now and deplore the misfortune of this alliance. It placed the leaders of the Church on the unpopular side of a quarrel not unlike that which four hundred years before the Church had fought for the people against the King. And it gave Puritanism the accidental advantage of espousing the cause which became in later days the cause of civil liberty. Strange that the Church which fought for the Magna Charta should have been placed in the attitude of defending the tyranny of royalty, and that a sect whose fundamental doctrine was the ultramontane denial of the rights of civil government should appear as the champion of constitutional liberty.

The political history of James' reign is the history of the development of the Parliamentary consciousness of its rights and of the Crown's blind determination not to recognize it. The King possessed neither the presence, nor the intellect, nor the courage, nor the personal popularity of the Tudors, and yet his claims were even more absolute and his public utterances more dictatorial. Elizabeth had recognized the growth of the parliamentary spirit, and after a severe struggle over the question of monopolies, had yielded to the Commons with her usual sagacity. But James was devoid of political wisdom and his four parliaments, one by one, were dissolved, each more discontented than the others. We are familiar with the Parliament's use of its financial authority to bring the King to terms; the popular excitement over the King's exercise of his prerogative in raising duties on imports and exports, and his vindication by the Court of Exchequer; his unwise challenge to popular prejudice in seeking a Spanish alliance; his sacrifice of Bacon and Raleigh, and devotion to the wretched Buckingham; his interference with the freedom of Parliamentary debate, and his disastrous attempt at war in the Palatinate, altogether the seed of a fearful harvest for his son to reap.

Ecclesiastically the reign promised well, but ended most unhappily. The Church had the ablest set of Bishops since the Reformation. Bancroft, and Andrewes, and Bilson would have done credit to any age, and the translation of the

Bible in 1611 is a lasting monument to the literary taste and judgment and scholarship of the time. The Puritans had receded from many of their extreme positions, and asked only the privilege of ministering in the Church without obeying the objectionable rubrics. Their " millenary petition," or " petition of a thousand," signed by 750 preachers, had little weight with the King, although he summoned representative Churchmen and Puritans to a Conference at Hampton Court in 1604. The record * of this conference is a fair illustration of the character of the King and the method and matter of the arguments on the opposing sides. The King showed his partiality and his vanity by naming more Churchmen than Puritans, and by largely conducting the disputation himself. Yet some of his arguments have so much shrewdness in them that we almost enjoy his interference. The Puritans offered the usual objections, with many trivial criticisms of the Prayer Book, as, for example, that in the XXIIId article it is said, " it is not lawful for anyone in the congregation to preach before he is lawfully called," and this might imply that " anyone out of the congregation might preach without being lawfully called." The King expressed his objection to adding any negative statements to the Articles, and said : " I think it unfit to thrust into

---

* Fuller, III. 172.

the book of Articles every position negative, which would swell the book into a volume as big as the Bible and confound the reader. Thus, one Mr. Craig, in Scotland, with his 'I renounce and abhor,' and his multiplied detestations and abrenunciations, so amazed simple folk that, not being able to conceive all these things, they fell back into Popery or remained in their former ignorance." Dr. Reynolds, who moderately pleaded for the Puritans, was the scholar of whom Fuller says that "he had been in early life a zealous Papist, whilst his brother William was as earnest a Protestant, and Providence so ordered it that by their mutual disputation John Reynolds turned an eminent Protestant and William an inveterate Papist." He was himself a strict Conformist, and although called a leader of the Puritans, it is characteristic of the times that on his dying bed he asked for and received the formal absolution of the Church.

The Hampton Court Conference left the King more than ever satisfied with his aphorism—" No Bishop, no King," and the Churchmen absurdly worshipful of his royal ability. The Puritans, not satisfied with the concessions made to them, began an earnest agitation for the ultimate triumph of their cause, by petitions and preaching, and by the gradual acquisition of influence in Parliament.

Archbishop Whitgift died in 1604 and was succeeded by Richard Bancroft, who proceeded on the same lines and with much the same determination. Finding that many of the clergy subscribed to the oath of obedience with internal reservations, he was authorized to enforce the *ex animo* test which compelled conscientious acquiescence and roused great opposition. Many of the Puritans were deprived, although from the conflicting accounts it is impossible to ascertain the number; and an agitation was begun in Parliament to compel the Bishops to cease enforcing obedience to the rubrics on the ground that this was the only way in which the vacant parishes could be supplied with ministers. Bancroft rightly or wrongly held that it was poor policy to fill the pulpits with men who ridiculed the method of public worship they were sworn to use. King James' resistance of this demand of Parliament was the beginning of his troubles.

Lord Clarendon in his "History of the Great Rebellion" praises the wisdom and efficiency of Bancroft's administration, and maintains that his policy of strict conformity was rapidly eliminating the obstructionist element from the Church, and so by combining the more zealous of the clergy and people was weakening the Puritan party. Certain it is that throughout this period there is growing complaint from the Puritans of the increasing popularity of the Church and her ceremonies *—although the stricter line between parties and the alienation of many who had hitherto conformed for the sake of peace, together with the fierce mutterings on the subject in Parliament, give the impression of the increased strength of the opposition.

The appointment of George Abbot to the primacy in 1611 was perhaps the very worst thing that could have happened to the Church. Whitgift and Bancroft had been at least consistent, but Abbot cannot be classified. The Bishops had agreed to recommend Launcelot Andrewes, who was in every way fitted for the position, but Abbot's flattery of the King and his court influence won the day. The new primate was a rigid Calvinist, a sympathizer with the Puritans, superficially learned, and narrow and morose in character. He showed his true Calvinistic temper by his persecution of heretics, two of whom were burnt the year after his accession, the first time such a thing had happened in England in forty years.† Under him and James together the Church was nearly committed to the Calvinistic decrees of the Synod of Dort and the pitiful persecution of Barnveldt and Hugo Grotius. It was the beginning of that discussion of predestination and free-will which gave a theological cast to the Puritan position. Abbot favored and consorted with

---

* Perry, 370.   † Perry, 388.

Puritans until many of the Bishops, looking to the King alone for support and direction, became so abject in their flattery and dependence that we read their letters with shame. True there was a new school springing up in the Universities, of which Laud was the chief spirit. But the times were too critical for gradual improvement. The laxity and indifference and unwisdom of a reign like that of Abbot's brought about a condition of things, the issue of which no power on earth could have prevented. Laud gave his life afterwards to this hopeless task—hopeless in so far as he himself did not live to see the result. That twenty-two years from Bancroft's death to Laud's accession is in some respects the saddest period in the history of the Church of England. Churchmen, blind to the signs of the times, wasted their energy in attacking Romanism which was powerless to harm them. The Archbishop fostered a negative and hazy Churchmanship which was sapping the strength of the Establishment in high places. It is the drifting of a bark without a pilot in a stormy sea, frightened by the distant prospect of Romanism and hugging the dangerous coast upon which it was fated to go to pieces.

When King James died in 1625, he left the Church weakened by the incompetency of its leaders, and the Puritans strong with the patronage and politic favor of a discontented Parliament.

There are two events of the reign which demand a more extended notice, as bearing upon matters of deep interest to Churchmen in our own day. The first is the publication in 1618 of the King's "Book of Sports," intended especially for the relief of the people of Lancashire, who appeared to the King to be subjected by the magistrates to an unnecessary and ill-advised restriction from all recreation on Sunday.* The book was republished in 1633 by order of Charles I., and roused the most terrific opposition because it contradicted the fundamental principle of Puritanism, which was the literal application of Old Testament precepts to the regulation of Christian conduct. To us the provisions of the book, certainly if intended for the poor and laboring classes, are not unreasonable. It was simply ordered that " between the hours of Divine Service which in no case should be let or hindered," lawful athletic recreations might be indulged in, provided there was nothing essentially inconsistent with the observance of the day, such as bear-baiting and bull-baiting and cruelties of like character. Such liberty appears to be sanctioned, as Dr. Hessey says,† by the general practice of the Church before the Reformation, and was never prohibited either by precept or example by the first reformers—neither by Calvin nor Cranmer, nor either, it would seem, by John

---

* Fuller, III. 270. † B. L., p. 198.

Knox himself. It may be that the confusion of the times led to an abuse of the privilege in the reign of Elizabeth, for the Puritan advocacy of a Sabbatarian strictness begins about 1580. The same view of religion which induced the Puritans to assert the obligation of the Mosaic law * in criminal cases so that idolaters or Papists, adulterers, witches, demoniacs, Sabbath-breakers and other offenders ought to be put to death, determined their conception of Sunday. To them the word Sunday had a heathenish sound. It was not found in the Bible. The Sabbath, with all its severity of judgments, did occur in that part of it to which they were most devoted. Accordingly they reasoned that they were bound by the Levitical ordinance, although not so strictly but that "one day in seven" might be substituted for the "seventh day." This interpretation satisfied all the difficulties which might arise from St. Paul's epistles. These floating opinions were reduced to a system in a book written by Dr. P. Bownd and published in 1595. He declares that the Mosaic law on the subject is moral and perpetual and forbids all levity on the Christian Sabbath, from "the ringing of two bells" to private conversation on pleasurable or worldly topics. It was nothing to him that the Church in every age had distinguished between the Jewish Sabbath and the Christian

---

* Cf. Hallam, C. H. I. 210.

festival, and the inference from the New Testament was disregarded. The ideas thus promulgated spread with great rapidity and were welcome to large numbers of people who in transition from one religion to another craved definite and decided changes. Their natural outcome among American Puritans is seen in the " Blue Laws " of Connecticut, and in the very logical and apparently unanswerable position taken by John Traske in England in 1618. This man argued that the observance of the first day of the week under a strict interpretation of the Jewish law was inconsistent and that if it was wrong to change the manner of observance, it was wrong to change the day. He accordingly founded a sect which substituted Saturday for Sunday and in many other respects conformed to the literal observance of Old Testament precepts. To us, as we recall the storm of abuse through which Laud and Charles I. had to pass in their opposition to this Sabbatarian view, it cannot but be a cause of devout thanksgiving that the Church of England has never committed herself to any man's theory on this subject, but has quietly followed in the footsteps of the Apostles and of the Catholic Church for eighteen centuries in celebrating "the Day of our Lord's Resurrection and the weekly earnest of our own"; teaching her people to reverence the great event which the day commemorates, and trusting an enlightened conscience more than written law: recognizing that all men are not alike either in disposition, in habit, in position or circumstances, and that while the Church's public and formal thanksgiving to God is not neglected, there may be various and lawful expression of our serious joy over " the day which the Lord hath made " for the good of all His children.

The second matter of special importance—important because it led ultimately to that league between Scotland and the Long Parliament which overthrew the Church and throne of England—was the consecration in 1610 of three Bishops for the Scotch Church. This measure, though pressed by the King, seems to have been fully sanctioned by the Scotch Assembly* which nominated the three Bishops to be consecrated. Indeed during the whole terrible and turbulent period of the Scotch Reformation from 1560 onwards—a movement which for barbarous violence has no parallel except perhaps in Switzerland—there had never been more than eight years when there was not a nominal or pseudo-Episcopacy. The eight years of Melville's Presbyterian government really ended in 1600.† During the two years following James was in correspondence with Bancroft, having already secured the passage of an act restoring the Bishops to parliament. In 1603 or 1604 a canon was passed by the

---
* Perry, 382.   † Lawton.

English Convocation ordering prayer to be said for the Church of Scotland which, considering the high views of Bancroft and Andrewes, the authors of the canon, may be taken as an indication that a genuine Episcopacy was about to be restored to that country. The unhistorical use of this canon to convict the English Church of official recognition of the validity of non-episcopal ordination, suggests the propriety of a brief consideration of the views of Episcopacy entertained by the reformers on the continent and in England. There can be no question as to the law of the English Church. That has been declared of late years by judicial decision. The statutes and formal doctrinal statements are unwavering from the beginning. "The Institution of a Christian Man," put forth in 1537[*] before the question of orders had arisen, is clear enough, though in Scholastic language. The Ordinal of 1549, which the Puritans interpreted as teaching Apostolical Succession, the twenty-third and thirty-sixth of the XXXIX. Articles, the Acts of Elizabeth, even the "Reformatio Legum," leave no room for doubt as to the Church's mind. It has been said that Whittingham, Dean of Durham in Elizabeth's reign, and Travers, preacher at the Temple, had neither of them received Episcopal ordination, and this is true. But Whittingham died while his trial was

---

[*] Formularies of Henry VIIIth's reign.

pending, and Travers was actually deprived for this violation of the law.* At the beginning of Elizabeth's reign a letter was received from Calvin requesting the Queen to take steps for holding a conference of all Protestants for the purpose of uniting them under a common government and discipline. To this the Council quietly replied through the Archbishop that they would take the matter under consideration, but that the English Church was determined to preserve her Episcopate which had come down to her from Joseph of Arimathea in British times before the Roman usurpation.† This was the English view of Episcopacy without any uncalled for criticism of other Christian bodies. The law of the English Church never wavered once. As for the personal views of the reformers themselves they are rather difficult to ascertain in the continuous shifting of their theological position, but are interesting in the light of modern discussion. Until 1532 the treatment of the subject of Holy Orders was evidently largely influenced by the Scholastic language. S. Thomas Aquinas expressed the views of the Schoolmen in his " Summa Theologiæ," where (Q. 40 and 41 Sup.), in order to emphasize the dignity of the priestly office and the supremacy of the Pope, he denies that the Episcopate is a separate order, although in other places

---

* Neale I. 145.   † Strype's Parker, I. 138.

he asserts the distinct superiority of Bishops in matters of government. The Papal claims were in constant conflict with the earlier doctrine of the Apostolical Succession so that John Gerson, Chancellor of the University of Paris, in 1410 * declares that the authority of the Episcopate had been so depreciated by the Papalists that they had left only "painted images of Bishops." As late as 1560 the Italian party in the Council of Trent succeeded in suppressing the true doctrine of the Apostolical Succession which had been urged by the Spanish and French Bishops.† To this we may add the enormous prominence given to the sacrificial aspect of the Eucharist, which created a desire to level the Episcopate down to the Priesthood, and it will be evident that the germ of later Protestant theories was found in Ultramontanism. Thus the earlier reformers started out with at best a maimed conception of the ministry which prepared them, deserted as they were by their Bishops, for the ultimate denial of the Episcopal succession, whenever a new theory of government should be boldly proclaimed. This tendency was increased by the popular identification of the Episcopal *régime* with Papal tyranny. As it was, however, Luther and Melancthon fairly longed for a restoration of Episcopacy,‡ and Bucer regarded it as established by the Holy

---

* Gies. iv. 131.   † Buckley.   ‡ Hardwick, p. 343 n.

Ghost.* The Augsburg confession itself accepts the government of Bishops, and whatever Erastianism colored Cranmer's wavering opinions he certainly had very high views of the ministry in 1548 and 1549 † just about the time when the preface to our Ordinal was written. In 1541 John Calvin, a French layman, never in Holy Orders, "flew to his funereal throne of Geneva" and began to teach that Bishops and Presbyters were originally of the same order, quoting the private opinion of S. Jerome.‡ His genius recognized that the Lutherans had crippled themselves by subjection to the State and he seized the accidental advantages offered him in Geneva to establish a system which became a considerable factor in our history. Calvin never denied the historical prestige and expediency of the Episcopal government—in one of his letters he recommends it to be adopted, and in his Commentary on Titus he admits its apostolic institution. Yet the Genevan Council of Presbyters gradually became to the continental reformers the model of all Church government, and it is amazing in the light of this history to hear the exclusive claims of this system so strongly asserted in Elizabeth's reign that there are several instances of English clergy going over to the Continent to be reordained by Calvin's successors on the ground that

---

* Bramhall. † Catechism, 1548. ‡ Institutes.

their previous ordination was invalid.* The dominion that Calvin claimed and exercised in the Protestant world of the sixteenth century has no parallel in history. It was dangerous to differ from him and his word was law. The generation of English Churchmen immediately succeeding Cranmer grew up under this influence. In Mary's reign they were indebted to the continental reformers for many offices of friendship, and they were drawn to them by the bond of a common persecution. Calvin, Bullinger and Beza gradually supplanted Luther and Melancthon as authorities in theology and the ancient Fathers were but superficially examined. For thirty years therefore there is an unsatisfactory vagueness and sometimes an Erastian indifference on the part of English Churchmen, even like Parker, in asserting the historic truth of Episcopacy. Most of them seem to have been satisfied to preserve the institution themselves without hazarding any opinion as to the continental Churches, holding, as Bramhall expressed it, that "it is charity to think well of our neighbors and good divinity to look well to ourselves." † The fiercer race of Puritans, recognizing the feebleness of this position, boldly opposed to it the positive, dogmatic claim of the divine obligation of Presbyterian government, and this was successfully resisted only when a new

---
* Neale, I. 144.   † III. 475.

generation of men like Bancroft, Bilson, Saravia and Andrewes dared to defend the Prayer Book theory of the ministry by an appeal to Scripture and antiquity—and to take a stand which, if not agreeable to the politicians, was at least defensible and consistent. Hooker, while carefully leaving a rather impracticable loophole of escape for his opponents in two hypothetical cases of special revelation and absolute necessity, shows no real doubt as to his own position. He was a pioneer—his great work was of an essentially tentative character, although some controversialists have endeavored vainly to find in him the final statement of the Anglican position. In Mr. Gardiner's words, "Hooker's greatness indeed . . . consisted rather in the entireness of his nature than in the thoroughness with which his particular investigations were carried out. . . . The work which had to be done by the generation which came after him was work which he could not do. . . . Men were to arise who in clearness of conception and in logical precision, surpassed the great Elizabethan writer as far as the political themes of Pym and Somers surpassed those of Elizabethan statesmen."*

The storm of political revolution was already gathering when Charles I. came to the throne of England in 1625. The gradual development

---

* I. 158 (cf. Perry).

of the royal power, largely emphasized by antagonism to the temporal claims of the Papacy and the decay of feudalism, had brought men face to face with the issue between absolutism in government and constitutional liberty. Spain and France had solved the problem in favor of pure despotism, and it was left to England to enter upon that terrific struggle which lasted over forty years, and which is in many respects the most important and the most deplorable in her annals. The movement was conducted not by the mass of the people, for it was not in the true sense popular, but by a group of prominent leaders who were not perfectly clear in their own minds as to the end in view, and who had hardly begun their work of political reform before they were overwhelmed, and driven and swept away by a riot of religious and political fanaticism which tore up the institutions of government and society from their foundations. Thus Churchmen like Hampden, Pym and Eliot sounded the note of civil freedom, and Puritans like Prynne and Peters and Cromwell swelled it into a blast of anarchy. The conflicting currents of thought and action during this period defy complete analysis. The elements of truth in all such national convulsions are to be judged only by their permanent results and two things survived the English rebellion. The principle of constitutional liberty was established in 1688 and the widespread reaction in favor of the old Church was the triumphant witness to the folly and fanaticism which had tried to confound religious with political questions. What the Church, trammelled as she was, had failed to accomplish by the unhappy use of the secular arm, was easily won by the glaring incompetence of the enemies who supplanted her.

The logic of events has forever demolished that theory of the divine right of kings for which Charles I. contended; but the most brilliant historian has failed in his effort to justify the proceedings of the Long Parliament or to convict the King of intentional injustice. Charles I. began his reign fettered, handicapped by a false and pernicious education which had filled him with a consciousness of the royal prerogative. That isolation which was pre-eminently in his day the curse of kings shut him off from any real knowledge of the feelings and the needs and wishes of his people, for Parliament was not yet truly representative. He was by nature weak and yielding. He lacked that enormous self-will which is the safety and shame of tyrants. He was not gifted with the bold shrewdness and unscrupulous craft which made Elizabeth's deception not only successful but respectable and gained for kings the reputation for statesmanship. His unskilful attempts at so-called diplomacy have excited the scorn of partial historians. His theory of royalty and his treatment of parliaments are the well-worn targets of modern ridicule. And yet there are thousands of men who deplore the strange and dreadful fury which made him its victim. His kingly dignity, his courage, the personal purity and gentleness of his private life, his love of art and literature, appeal still to many men who pity his weakness in sacrificing Strafford, and compassionate the enforced ignorance and hereditary blindness which failed to read the signs of the times; and admire the devotion with which, in spite of wife and friends, he clung to the Church he loved and went calmly to his death. He was at his best when he stood upon the scaffold. As even Macaulay is forced to say: "The captive King, retaining all his regal dignity and confronting death with dauntless courage, gave utterance to the feelings of his oppressed people, manfully refused to plead before a court unknown to the law, appealed from military violence to the principles of the constitution, asked by what right the House of Commons had been purged of its most respectable members and the House of Lords deprived of its legislative functions, and told his weeping hearers that he was defending not only his cause but theirs . . . and thus his enemies gave him an opportunity of displaying at the last on a great theatre before the eyes of all nations and ages some qualities which irresistibly call forth the admiration and love of mankind, the high spirit of a gallant gentleman and the patience and meekness of a penitent Christian."

The history of the Church from 1630 to 1644 is the life of William Laud, successively President of S. John's College, Oxford, Bishop of London and Archbishop of Canterbury. It has taken two-hundred and fifty years for the smoke of bitter controversy and unscrupulous abuse to clear away, and even now historians are only beginning to do him simple justice. It is hardly to be expected that those who deny the truth of his religious position will find anything attractive in him. But any Churchman who regards Christianity as an historical inheritance; whose sympathy is roused and his zeal inflamed by the memory of the Church's continuous organic life; anyone who rejects the theory that religion is the mere product of the individual or collective consciousness of any age or generation—he must find in Laud, not perfection perhaps, not freedom from all fault and weakness, but an example of heroic unselfishness as honest and as fearless as any which the English Church has produced. The reckless and unlimited abuse which his enemies have heaped upon him is the best contradiction of their repeated statement that he was not a great man.

Laud was fifteen years old when Bancroft

preached his famous sermon at St. Paul's Cross in 1589 and the full tide of the earnest Churchmanship of that era swept his heart away with it. One idea took possession of him—mind and soul. He dreamed of a Church which should be truly Catholic; which should be loyal to those fundamental principles of faith and order which had conquered the heathenism of Rome and had survived the contention and abuse of fifteen centuries. A Church which should be too broad, he said, to bind men's minds in the specific and narrow doctrinal tyranny of either the Romanist or the Puritan; which should be a patron of art, of literature, of science, and yet be faithful to all that was truest and noblest in her venerable past. To this idea Laud devoted all his time, his energy, his learning. He saw the Church drifting into a narrow and immoral Calvinistic conception of God, with its theory of an invisible and unknowable Church and unreal sacraments. He saw the Romanist on the one hand and the Puritan on the other pledged to accomplish the Church's ruin, and men in high place who had been enriched by her spoil encouraging that fanaticism. At Oxford men called him an Arminian and a Romanist. They scoffed at his reverence and reviled at his doctrine. The leader of the Puritans taunted him with being a poor man's son and the chief of the Romanists sneered at his mad theory of the

Church's Catholicity. He was always calm, unruffled and persistent. His learning vanquished his opponents when his patience did not disarm them. He made his way through a very thicket of curses and contempt, and he lived to find himself, in spite of almost unnumbered obstacles, Bishop of London at the age of fifty-five and Archbishop of Canterbury at sixty-one. During all these years he had not wavered for an instant The idea of the Church in the breadth, fulness and richness of her life and beauty—that idea had mastered and possessed him. As Archbishop of Canterbury he had the power he thought to realize something of his dream. The King was no longer an Erastian Tudor but himself religiously loyal to the Church, and Laud saw in the legal authority of the Archiepiscopal office an instrument for the accomplishment of his purpose. He used the High Commission Court as he found it and for the existence of which he was not responsible. He increased and enlarged his power by personal influence. He rebuked the King for disregard of the proprieties of public worship. He converted the frivolous Buckingham to his views. He roused the poorer clergy to something like enthusiasm. He threw himself perhaps unwisely into the political life of the nation and mastered every detail of its commerce and manufacture. The greatest minds of the Church owed their encouragement or elevation to him,—Jeremy Taylor, Sanderson, Bramhall, Heylin, Herbert, Hammond, Chillingworth. He fought Romanism with unprecedented success because he stood on solid, historic ground, and the Pope took the mean revenge of offering him a Cardinal's hat in order to rouse against him the reckless hatred of his enemies. The Puritans said that he had no religion because for this great dream of his life he consented to mix with the courtly crowd and busy himself with State questions of the time. Yet beneath all this busy, terrifically exciting, superficial life, his diary showed that he *was* religious—religious after the old fashion, the religion of the hair-shirt and leathern girdle—in bitter penitence, in strict self-denial, in hours of private agony and rapture of prayer, in glad study of Holy Scripture. Little he thought that some of his enemies whose religion consisted largely in confident assurance of their freedom from sin and certainty of salvation, would drag out these expressions of penitence from his diary and torture them into an admission of heinous crime. He did not know or seem to realize that it was too late; that complications had arisen which rendered a struggle for the Church unequal; that Puritanism was too completely organized to be easily overthrown. The Archbishop made himself unpopular. At the King's desire he approved and encouraged the introduction of liturgical worship into the Scotch Church where an Episcopal government was smothered by a Calvinistic machinery. He dared to rebuke the nobles for their immoral and unchristian living. He dared to insist upon the Church's right to her own incomes and to take the part of the poorer and lower clergy and to censure Bishops for living in luxury in London when their dioceses were neglected. He dared to be accessible always to the poor and the oppressed, to give them lavishly of his income, to dress plainly, to avoid ostentation and to protest against the fanaticism, the narrowness of Puritanism, and to assert the native healthfulness and brightness of the English character. He offended that class of land-owners who controlled Parliament and who never forgave him for making his way to high office in the Church. Above all he refused to permit men who voluntarily took the vows in the Ordinal to contradict the Prayer Book in all their services: for of one thing he was certain—that the Prayer Book, whatever else it was, had never been a Puritan book and until it should be changed it ought to be obeyed.

They said that he was an innovator and he was. He repaired the old Cathedral windows which had been broken down, and he loved the dignity and grandeur of a ceremonial service. He found the communion table in churches a mockery and a disgrace.* "Churchwardens kept their accounts

---
* Quoted by Mozley.

on it; parishioners despatched parish business at it; schoolmasters taught their boys to write at it; boys had their hats, satchels and books upon it; men sat on it and leant on it at sermon time, and glaziers knocked it full of nail holes." He did resent this, as even the Puritan Abbot had done before him,* and he ordered that the table should be placed close to the wall against the east end of the church and railed off from the congregation with a "railing close enough to keep out the dogs." That was all. He did practise acts of reverence and encourage men to do so, but I do not find them in the published orders. In fact as we read Bishop Wren's "orders and directions," put out with Laud's sanction, and the charges made against him at his trial, we are astonished at his moderation. Laud was not hated chiefly for his ceremonialism. He was hated because he believed in the Catholicity and historical continuity of the Church; because he refused to permit the XXXIX. Articles to be interpreted in the interest of the extremest Calvinism and the whole tone and teaching of the Prayer Book to be ignored. He was hated finally because in every position he took he seemed to be so resolutely successful. As he said boldly at his trial: "Whatever I did, I did to the uttermost of my knowledge, according to both law and canon and with the consent and

---

* Cardwell, II. 227.

liking of the people; nor did any command issue out from me against the one or without the other that I know of."

Every man has his failings and Laud's lack of tact and policy, his care for little things, his straightforward resoluteness and invincible determination won for him the reputation of being bigoted, foolish, superstitious and narrow-minded. The best modern criticism, even that which is unfriendly, does him more justice and contents itself with saying that he was pure, unselfish, even ascetic in his private life, that he was by nature a lover of order and discipline, "devoid of the higher spiritual enthusiasm" which characterizes greater minds. He was devoid of that "higher spiritual enthusiasm" which would attempt an uncertain union of the Church by the surrender of the fundamental principles upon which her life had rested for one thousand five hundred years. His bitterest enemy admitted that his defence before Parliament was able, learned and complete and that there was no law under which he could be convicted. And so he died—the old man in his seventy-third year. Or as he expressed it, he passed through the red-sea—the sea of blood—with the same calm and cheerful trust in God which had characterized him all his life and which provoked his tormenters into a brutality of petty cruelty upon the scaffold,— a cheerfulness which some count madness and others know to be the assurance of faith. As Professor Mozley says: "Laud saved the English Church"—saved her from being choked with the iron chain of Calvinism and made it possible that men with Catholic convictions could live within her fold.

The history of the long parliament demonstrates the deadly effect of all these years of religious strife. The parliament was composed almost entirely of Churchmen, but Churchmen of three classes. There were those who sympathized with Laud and who regarded the Church as their Catholic heritage and reverenced its sacraments and its services. There were others, including many of the nobility and gentry who owed their place and fortunes to Tudor times, who regarded the Church as a department of the State and were satisfied with the expediency of Episcopal government if it could be easily and consistently maintained. And finally there were Churchmen who were infected with Calvinistic doctrine and who secretly longed for further reformation in the direction of the Genevan model, and who had conformed to the Prayer Book rather from policy than conviction. Neither of these two latter classes of Churchmen were capable of resisting the strain of political necessity.

Parliament in 1606 fought King James and declared that the Scots were beggars, rebels, traitors;

that there had not been a single King of Scotland who had not been murdered by his subjects, and that it was as reasonable to unite England and Scotland as it would be to place a prisoner at the bar on an equality with a judge upon the bench.* And Parliament in 1643, alarmed for its own safety in the civil war against the King, abandoned the Church in order to get assistance from the Scotch and bound itself by the "Solemn league and and covenant" to extirpate Prelacy and to submit to Presbyterianism. Thus Puritanism won the day and began a seventeen years' reign of religious intolerance and confusion without a precedent in English history. Prelacy was abolished. Calvinism was adopted. A Directory of worship was published. All holidays were forbidden—all religious services at funerals were condemned. The use of the Prayer Book in public or in private was prohibited and a penalty imposed of a fine of £5 for the first offence and imprisonment for the second, and this was afterwards extended to a recitation of the prayers from memory. Walker, on p. 198 of his book on "The Sufferings of the Clergy," demonstrates with abundant evidence that about 8,000 of the English clergy, most of them with their wives and children, were ejected from their livings, notwithstanding numerous petitions from their parishioners, and left without means of sup-

---

* Skottowe, p. 63.

port. Some fled to the continent, many were imprisoned, some starved to death, and negotiations were entered into for disposing of some of them by selling them into slavery. Churches were desecrated, and art galleries and monuments destroyed. Horses and swine were baptized in mockery in the Cathedral fonts. S. Paul's became a stable for horses, and Westminster Abbey was turned into a barrack. Within two years sixteen sects sprang up which vied with each other in the active encouragement of misrule. Arguments against toleration were put forth by the Presbyterian party which anathematized schism and maintained that it was grievous sin to separate from their true Church. But Cromwell and his army put an end to this tyranny and established a system of government which was forced to be tolerant to all sects except Churchmen, Roman Catholics, Quakers and Unitarians. Thus both religiously and politically the rebellion was a failure. Once indeed the Lord Protector permitted a free election, and the Parliament of 1654 is known as the first Parliament representing the United Kingdom; but its early dissolution proved that constitutional government was impossible, and Cromwell did not dare to trust again to a free election.

Religiously the government was a parody, and the great mass of the people were indignantly restive under this new Papalism and longed for the Church's restoration. When that came in 1660, the reformation of the Church of England may be said to have been completed. The conflict had been for one hundred years on the interpretation of the Prayer Book, and the Church's revision in 1662 settled that question by finally deciding in favor of Laud as against the Puritans.

The years that have passed since the Great Rebellion have removed much bitterness, and sobered men's judgments and taught them many lessons of breadth, of wisdom, of toleration. The ideal Puritan with his gloomy solemnity, his relentless determination, his peculiarities of manner, of dress, and conversation; his exquisite assumption of right to examine into other men's consciences; his enormous assurance, his passionate zeal for a narrow and Judaic conception of Christianity—has passed away from amongst us. What was true and abiding in that for which he contended is with us still. For the present contains the harvest of all the past and the seed of all the future, and history is but the record of God's dealings with His people, whereby He has brought good out of apparent evil and has vindicated the truth of that unchangeable law of righteousness to which all human actions must ultimately be adjusted.

Puritanism has been regarded by many as a

necessary factor in the growth of that civil liberty with which at the Rebellion it was accidentally associated. But nothing can be clearer, reinforced as it is by the history of New England, than that not only was there no essential connection between that peculiar form of reformed Christianity and our modern freedom; but that some of its axioms were as contradictory to our modern conceptions of the proper relations between Church and State as were the theories of Hildebrand and Innocent III.

Puritanism as a system must be judged by its immediate results. It must be looked at, as it was,—not glorified by the characters of individual men who in later days have owned hereditary allegiance to it; not as modified and altered to meet new conditions and adapted to the more liberal and enlighted conceptions of our modern world. The Puritanism we have been considering had its results to be seen and read of all men. As Matthew Arnold[*] says, " The triumph of the Puritan conception and presentation of righteousness was so at war with the ancient and inbred integrity, piety and good nature and good humor of the English people, that it led straight to moral anarchy, to the profligacy of the Restoration. It led to the court, the manners, the stage, the literature which we know. It led to the

---

[*] Essay on Falkland, p. 170.

long discredit of serious things, to the dryness of the 18th century, to the irreligion which vexed Butler's righteous soul, the aversion and incapacity for all deep inquiries concerning religion and its sanctions, to the belief so frequently found now among the followers of natural science that such inquiries are unprofitable."

It checked and cramped that intellectual and literary development which was the glory of Elizabeth's reign. An alien in every sense, by birth and by adoption, it has been a source of discord to the English Church—choking the freedom of her growth and deadening her spiritual power—breeding that widespread and unhappy dissension and disunion which is the present agony of the English-speaking Protestant world.

www.ingramcontent.com/pod-product-compliance
Lightning Source LLC
Chambersburg PA
CBHW032000230426
43672CB00010B/2219